MR. & MRS. SPARKES

Six One Act Plays

by Mabel Constanduros
and Howard Agg

FOR PRODUCTION ENQUIRIES

UNITED KINGDOM AND WORLD
EXCLUDING NORTH AMERICA
licensing@concordtheatricals.co.uk

020-7054-7298

NORTH AMERICA
info@concordtheatricals.com
1-866-979-0447

Each title is subject to availability from Concord Theatricals, depending upon country of performance.

photocopying, recording, videotaping, or otherwise, without the prior written permission of the publisher. No one shall share this title, or part of this title, to any social media or file hosting websites.

The moral right of Mabel Constanduros and Howard Agg to be identified as author of this work has been asserted in accordance with Section 77 of the Copyright, Designs and Patents Act 1988.

USE OF COPYRIGHTED MUSIC

A licence issued by Concord Theatricals to perform this play does not include permission to use the incidental music specified in this publication. In the United Kingdom: Where the place of performance is already licensed by the PERFORMING RIGHT SOCIETY (PRS) a return of the music used must be made to them. If the place of performance is not so licensed then application should be made to PRS for Music (www.prsformusic.com). A separate and additional licence from PHONOGRAPHIC PERFORMANCE LTD (www.ppluk.com) may be needed whenever commercial recordings are used. Outside the United Kingdom: Please contact the appropriate music licensing authority in your territory for the rights to any incidental music.

USE OF COPYRIGHTED THIRD-PARTY MATERIALS

Licensees are solely responsible for obtaining formal written permission from copyright owners to use copyrighted third-party materials (e.g., artworks, logos) in the performance of this play and are strongly cautioned to do so. If no such permission is obtained by the licensee, then the licensee must use only original materials that the licensee owns and controls. Licensees are solely responsible and liable for clearances of all third-party copyrighted materials, and shall indemnify the copyright owners of the play(s) and their licensing agent, Concord Theatricals Ltd., against any costs, expenses, losses and liabilities arising from the use of such copyrighted third-party materials by licensees.

IMPORTANT BILLING AND CREDIT REQUIREMENTS

If you have obtained performance rights to this title, please refer to your licensing agreement for important billing and credit requirements.

INTRODUCTION

The following plays are six little events that happen to Mr. and Mrs. Sparkes, a quiet, domesticated couple living in a small suburban house near London.

They all take place in the little sitting-room of the Sparkes' house. It is a neat, bright, soulless-looking room, furnished in fumed oak and deep fawn moquette with splashes of brown: quite pleasant and comfortable but, like hundreds of its kind, entirely without character.

Up R. is the door, with below it the fireplace. On each side of the fireplace is an easy chair, and beside the one up stage is a rack with books and papers in it. Opposite the fireplace are french windows leading out to the small garden. Below the french windows is a small table on which is the telephone. Another table, circular in shape, is in the centre of the room. Against the back wall is a cabinet holding books in one section and a hugger-mugger assortment of cheap china ornaments in the other. There are one or two familiar prints on the walls—such as "The Soul's Awakening" and "Wedded" —in nice brown frames picked out with gold. Also, there is a picture of Mr. Sparkes's mother and Mrs. Sparkes's father in similar frames. Here and there, dotted about the room, are little pieces of pottery and brass which Mr. and Mrs. Sparkes have picked up on their holidays; and over the fireplace are a handsome pair of antlers which they bought recently at a second-hand shop—because they like antlers.

* * * * *

As Mr. and Mrs. Sparkes figure in each play, and Mrs. Bocking and the Inspector in others, it will be as well to describe them here, at the beginning:

MR. NELSON SPARKES is a little man: kind, meek and tolerant— except, occasionally, with his wife, when he can be quite surprisingly terse and dominating. He speaks very precisely and lends to every topic of conversation—be it the weather, gardening, or the morning train—a serious consideration that is most impressive, though in anyone else it would seem a little comic. He is very contented with

3

his lot in life, which is that of a traveller in a cheese firm. He has no sense of humour, but in spite of it manages to be likeable.

MRS. SPARKES—or "Mummie"—is quiet, gentle and unobtrusive, and always very conscious of her husband's superiority, which one doesn't suppose she has ever thought of questioning. She listens with awe and admiration to his exploits in the big world of Cheese and Commerce into which he is whisked every morning by the 8.35 train, and thinks how noble and clever he is. Sometimes she is a little fussy in her over-eagerness to keep him healthy and comfortable, and this annoys him: also her grasp of a subject can be very feeble, due to her almost complete credulity, and this annoys him even more. But what are these tiny flaws, he often asks himself, in a wife who is in every other way "a treasure"?

MRS. BOCKING is a gaunt, sharp-featured lady with an acid tongue and a genius for gossip. Beside her Mummie presents the spectacle of a chirping little wren against a swooping hawk. She lives next door to the Sparkeses.

THE INSPECTOR—her brother—is a powerful-looking man with a brusque, down-to-business manner and a sharp eye. But there is a kind look in his face. He always wears plain clothes and an overcoat and carries his hat in his hand all the time he is on the stage.

*　*　*　*　*

There are other characters in the plays, but they will best be described as and when they appear.

PLAYS

These plays were first produced by the British Broadcasting Corporation, commencing June 16th, 1941, with the following casts:

Nelson Sparkes	Richard Goolden.
Mummie	Mabel Constanduros.
Mrs. Booking	Phylis Morris.
Sydney Carter	Jack Livesey.
Nurse Schofield	Muriel Aked.
The Sailor	Carl Bernard.
Inspector	Arthur Young.
Aunt Rebecca	Dora Gregory.
Sharpe	John Bryning.
Alice	Betty Hardy.

Plays produced by Mary Allen.

THE WHITE RUSSIAN*

CHARACTERS

NELSON SPARKES.
MUMMIE.
MRS. BOOKING.
INSPECTOR.

When the CURTAIN *rises it is just after lunch on a Saturday afternoon, and* MR. SPARKES *is sitting in his chair by the fire (the one up stage) stooping down to tie the laces of his gardening shoes. He is wearing an old tweed jacket, which he always uses to garden in, with a pair of dark trousers turned up well over his shoes to prevent them getting dirtied.*

The door of the room is open and in a moment MUMMIE *comes in. She has on a summer frock of a rather drab, lifeless material with a necklace of cheap glass beads.*

MUMMIE. Oh, ducksie, would you like a cup of tea before you go in the garden? It'll freshen you up.

NELSON. No, dear, I'm afraid I haven't time. I've got a big afternoon in front of me. I'm sticking the peas, you know.

MUMMIE. Are you, dear? How exciting.

NELSON. Oh, Mummie, I forgot! How stupid of me. (*He puts his hand in his pocket.*)

MUMMIE. What, dear?

NELSON. Your birthday present. I meant to give it you at lunch and I forgot all about it.

MUMMIE. Not another one, dear? You gave me a lovely cake of soap last week. Don't you remember?

NELSON. Ah, but Nelson's been an extravagant boy. Look! (*He hands her, with some ceremony, a small paper packet.*)

MUMMIE (*taking it gingerly*). What is it?

NELSON. Open it carefully and you'll see.

(MUMMIE *begins to unwrap first a layer of brown paper, then tissue paper, then more tissue paper, finally revealing a little cardboard box.*)

MUMMIE (*opening it*). I can't think what it is.

* Please see page 6.

NELSON. I hope you'll like it.

MUMMIE (*the box is open—her eyes shining*). Oh, ducksie! A brooch! That isn't for me?

NELSON. Yes.

MUMMIE. Oh, but—it isn't a real emerald?

NELSON. Well, Mummie, that's not a very nice thing to say. Don't you like the brooch?

MUMMIE (*taking the brooch out of the box and holding it up*). Like it! I shall never dare to wear it. I never *saw* such a stone. Look at the way it catches the light. (*With sudden concern.*) Nelson. You're—all right, aren't you?

NELSON. Quite, dear. Except that cheese always rises a little, you know. Why?

MUMMIE. Because, Nelson, if this emerald's real it must have cost —well—pounds and pounds.

NELSON. I expect it did when the Czar bought it.

MUMMIE. The Czar! Not of Russia?

NELSON. Yes, dear. There isn't a Czar of anywhere else.

MUMMIE. But, ducksie, you didn't know the Czar.

NELSON. No, dear; but to-day I met a white Russian who did.

MUMMIE. A white what, dear?

NELSON. Russian. You know, dear, some Russians *were* white.

MUMMIE. Oh, were they? And what colour were the others?

NELSON. I'm afraid I forgot to ask him. You see, he was so busy telling me about the Crown Jewels. His mother brought a lot of them out of Russia.

MUMMIE. Why, dear?

NELSON. Well, dear, you see, she was a friend of the Czar's, and he lent her his silver aeroplane to escape from Russia.

MUMMIE. Who, dear?

NELSON. His mother.

MUMMIE. Whose mother, dear? You're muddling me.

NELSON. The white Russian's.

MUMMIE. Oh. You see, dear, you hadn't told me before that he had a mother.

NELSON. Well, Mummie, everyone has a mother.

MUMMIE. Unless they're orphans, dear.

NELSON. Well, he wasn't. When his mother was flying in the Czar's silver aeroplane over the sea, another aeroplane started to chase them.

MUMMIE. There!

NELSON. And this white Russian's mother, who was a very impetuous lady, leaned out of the aeroplane window to shake her fist——

MUMMIE. Fancy.

NELSON. No, dear, it's not fancy—it's true. She shook her fist so hard that all the Crown Jewels fell into the sea, except the Grand Duchess Sonia's emerald brooch.

MUMMIE. And why didn't that drop too, dear?

NELSON (*in a low voice*). Well, dear, to tell you the truth, it—fell down her corsage.

MUMMIE (*understandingly*). Oh! Oh, I see.

NELSON. Poor fellow, it was all that was left between him and starvation.

MUMMIE. What? The corsage?

NELSON. No, the brooch. He was so hungry, Mummie, he'd have taken anything for it. All he asked me was twenty-five shillings. I gave him twenty-five-and-six.

MUMMIE. Quite right to be generous, dear. (*Putting the brooch back in the box, and laying the box down on the table in the centre of the room.*) I think I'd better put it away at once. It's far too valuable to wear. Put your scarf on, dear, if you're going to garden. It was sweet of you, ducksie. You might easily have spent that twenty-five-and-six on that stuffed seagull you wanted so much.

NELSON (*going to the french windows*). It had gone, dear. I asked. (*Suddenly stopping—looking out.*) Mummie! Look out of the window. There's a dog walking right over my lettuces. Oh, that is too bad. Grrr! Booo! (*He waves his hands.*) People have no right to let their dogs tromple over other people's gardens. (*Calling out.*) Hi! H! Call off your dog! It's trompling on my garden. Mr. Brown!

(*He vanishes through the open french windows, still calling.*)

MUMMIE (*calling after him*). Ducksie! You've forgotten your scarf. Oh dear, oh dear . . .

(*A bell rings in the house.*)

Now, I wonder who that is, and the lunch not cleared away.

(*She crosses to the door and goes out into the hall. Her voice in the hall.*)

Oh, it's you, Mrs. Booking. Do come in, won't you?

MRS. BOOKING (*coming in*). So sorry to trouble you, Mrs. Sparkes, but could I borrow half a teacupful of flour?

MUMMIE. Certainly. Sit down while I get it.

MRS. BOOKING. Thank you.

MUMMIE (*going towards the door*). Do excuse the mess I'm in. Mr. Sparkes got back rather late. You know what men are : the later they are, the longer they take over their meals.

MRS. BOOKING. You don't need to tell me anything about men

being late for meals, my dear. You ought to live with my brother—he's an inspector at Scotland Yard, you know. What he costs me in gas hotting up his meals, I simply daren't tell you. (*Suddenly and in quite a different voice.*) My dear. Whatever's this on the table? (*She has caught sight of the brooch lying in the box on the table.*)

MUMMIE (*by her side*). Oh, it's only a little birthday present.

MRS. BOOKING (*slowly and meditatively*). An emerald half-moon brooch set in diamonds. (*Quickly.*) Where did you get that?

MUMMIE. My naughty extravagant husband bought it for me.

MRS. BOOKING. Bought it? Where?

MUMMIE. From a Russian—a white one.

MRS. BOOKING. When?

MUMMIE. To-day. He's just given it to me. Why?

MRS. BOOKING (*impressively*). Have you read to-day's papers?

MUMMIE. No. What with it being Saturday and Mr. Sparkes coming home to dinner and all the shopping, I haven't had a moment.

MRS. BOOKING. Then you don't know about the burglary?

MUMMIE. What burglary?

MRS. BOOKING. Last night. Old Mrs. Crawley. You know, lives in the big white house in its own grounds on the main road—or did live. Broke in, my dear, just before midnight, bashed her on the head with a blunt instrument, and took all her jewels.

MUMMIE. Oh dear. How dreadful! So near here, too. Doesn't make you feel very safe, does it? I'm glad I didn't know, because Mr. Sparkes was out till nearly one o'clock last night.

MRS. BOOKING (*darkly*). Your husband was out till one o'clock last night?

MUMMIE. Yes, he was entertaining a customer. He has to, sometimes, you know, when they buy a lot of his cheeses. They went to a music-hall.

MRS. BOOKING. H'mm. . . . Did you happen to see the programme?

MUMMIE. No, I don't think he brought it home. But he sang a lot of the songs. He was very lively. He can be very comical when he likes, you know.

MRS. BOOKING (*with portentous gravity*). Mrs. Sparkes, far be it from me to plant suspicion where none is, but the most valuable piece stolen from poor Mrs. Crawley last night was an emerald half-moon brooch set in diamonds.

MUMMIE. Really? If you'll just sit down I'll fetch the half-teacupful of flour——

MRS. BOOKING (*with feeling*). Down in this house, Mrs. Sparkes, I cannot sit.

MUMMIE. But why not, Mrs. Booking? There's nothing the matter with you, is there?

MRS. BOCKING. Don't try to throw wool in my eyes, Mrs. Sparkes.

MUMMIE. Throw wool? What *do* you mean?

MRS. BOCKING. It's no good your seeking to prevaricate with me, Mrs. S. I know all.

MUMMIE. But what do you know, Mrs. Bocking?

MRS. BOCKING. My poor woman, do you mean to say you don't see?

MUMMIE. See what?

MRS. BOCKING (*very darkly and slowly*). The most valuable piece of jewellery stolen from Mrs. Crawley last night was an emerald half-moon brooch set in diamonds.

MUMMIE (*with a gasp—her hands to her face*). *Mrs. Bocking ! !*

MRS. BOCKING. When I came in and laid my eyes on that brooch, you could have knocked me down with a feather.

MUMMIE. But Mr. Sparkes bought it, Mrs. Bocking. He told me so.

MRS. BOCKING. You'd take the word of a burglar?

MUMMIE. Oh, Mrs. Bocking, don't say such things about my husband.

MRS. BOCKING. My poor soul, I know what a dreadful shock it must be. I mean, *you* didn't know you were marrying a burglar, did you?

MUMMIE. Of course not. And he isn't.

MRS. BOCKING. Oh? Then how do you account for the presence of Mrs. Crawley's brooch on your dining-room table?

MUMMIE (*pitifully*). I've told you, Mrs. Bocking, Mr. Sparkes bought it off a white Russian.

MRS. BOCKING. I don't care if he *said* he bought it off a black Zulu.

MUMMIE. But he did. He even told me the price. It was twenty-five shillings.

MRS. BOCKING. For that! (*Quietly.*) My poor deluded creature, d'you know how much that emerald's worth? Ten thousand pounds.

MUMMIE. Oh, how dreadful! (*She sinks down into a chair by the table.*)

MRS. BOCKING (*towering over her*). D'you suppose any Russian, whatever colour he was, would sell it for twenty-five shillings? No, Mrs. Sparkes. I'm afraid you'll have to face it—unpleasant as it's going to be. Your husband is a secret burglar.

MUMMIE (*faintly*). Oh no!

MRS. BOCKING. And not only that—a manslaughterer, too.

MUMMIE. Oh, don't!

MRS. BOCKING. I'm only being cruel to be kind. What time did you say he came home last night?

MUMMIE (*with a gasp*). After one.

MRS. BOCKING. And Mrs. Crawley met her end at twelve-thirty. He came straight home to you—*red-handed*.

MUMMIE (*moaning*). Oh! Oh! Oh!

MRS. BOCKING. I don't wonder you're upset. So should I be. (*Ominously.*) You don't like to think of to-night, do you? Boxed up here in this little house alone with (*through her clenched teeth*)—a murderer.

MUMMIE (*desperately*). Oh, but, Mrs. Bocking, it can't be right. Mr. Sparkes wouldn't hurt a fly. He's such a harmless little man.

MRS. BOCKING. So was Crippen—at first. So was Charlie Peace—apparently. Played the violin. Took the plate round at church.

MUMMIE. But Nelson's so kind.

MRS. BOCKING. A very bad sign. So was that man at Liverpool. Twenty-five years he lived with his wife, a devoted husband; then one night he simply spread her on the hearthrug with a poker. (*Sharply.*) How long have you been married?

MUMMIE (*almost incoherent*). Twenty-five—years!

MRS. BOCKING. Then there's no time to be lost. He's broken out once; he'll do it again. Blood lust. Same with them all. He doesn't play the violin, by any chance?

MUMMIE (*tearfully*). No.

MRS. BOCKING. He will. Has he ever suggested having a kiln in the garden to burn rubbish?

MUMMIE. No.

MRS. BOCKING. Well, if he does, put your foot down and don't let him—because *you'll* be the rubbish.

MUMMIE. Oh, I can't believe it! I can't believe it! (*She is distraught.*)

MRS. BOCKING. Neither did Landru's wives till they went up in smoke.

MUMMIE (*wailing*). Oh dear, oh dear, oh dear!

MRS. BOCKING. Now, don't you worry. I don't suppose he'll do any harm before to-night. (*Cheerfully.*) I mean, he's probably sated with killing for the time being. But I'll have him under lock and key before the craze comes on again, don't you fear. I'll get my brother from Scotland Yard on to this. I'll go straight home now and ring him up.

MUMMIE. But I don't want Nelson under lock and key.

MRS. BOCKING. Then you ought to. Have you no public feeling? You don't want him running loose burgling and murdering all over the place, do you? Why, after he's done you in, he may turn on me. (*At the french window, darkly.*) Look at him out there in the garden, digging away as harmless-*looking* as a curate. Yet who knows the foul thoughts that may be festering behind those spectacled eyes? It's dreadful, isn't it?

MUMMIE. You mustn't say those things. You make me frightened.

MRS. BOOKING. I don't wonder. I wouldn't be you for anything. Don't let him prepare any food for you whatever you do—not even a cup of tea. He may take to poison for a change. Here he comes towards the house, carrying a spade, too. Look at the loving way he's stroking that sharp edge. It makes you shiver, doesn't it? I'm going. Don't trouble about the half-teacupful of flour, thank you, dear. I couldn't pat up a cake this afternoon if you were to pay me.

NELSON (*from the garden outside*). Mummie!——

(MRS. SPARKES *gives a petrified look in the direction of the garden.*)

MRS. BOOKING. I'm off. (*Pausing at the door.*) Remember— scream if you want me—*if* you get time.

(*She disappears and a second later we hear the front door bang as she leaves the house.*)

NELSON (*coming in through the french windows*). Mummie.
MUMMIE (*rooted to her chair—tremulously*). Y-yes, dear?
NELSON. I've been thinking. Don't you think it would be a good idea if we had an incinerator in the garden?
MUMMIE (*startled—gripping the arms of her chair*). What's that?
NELSON. It's a sort of small kiln, dear, for burning rubbish. You know, I believe I could knock one up myself if I bought a few bricks.
MUMMIE (*jumping up*). No! No! No! I won't have it!
NELSON. Mummie, what *is* the matter? Why shouldn't we have an incinerator?
MUMMIE (*terrified—shrinking away from him*). Because I don't want one.
NELSON. Are you quite well?
MUMMIE (*the only thing she can think of*). I—I—think I've got indigestion. (*She lays her hand on her heart.*)
NELSON. That's the cheese. I knew it wasn't ripe. Sit down and I'll make you a nice cup of tea, shall I?
MUMMIE (*more terrified—almost shouting*). No!
NELSON. Oh, very well, dear. Very well. You generally do like a cup of tea when you're not feeling quite the thing. (*He goes to the fireplace and takes up the poker.*) Fancy, Mummie, I was just thinking out there in the garden that it's twenty-five years to-day since we were married.
MUMMIE (*hoarsely—almost with her back against the door*). Put— down—that—poker.
NELSON (*turning to face her—the poker raised in his hand*). What, dear? I was going to knock down a nail in my shoe.
MUMMIE. I asked you to put the poker down. I——

(*There is a knocking on the front door.*)

NELSON (*putting down the poker*). Now, who's that? If it's the vicar, dear, I shall go out in the garden again. I'm too grubby to talk to him. I'll just have a look and make sure. (*He goes over to the french windows and peeps out sideways.* MUMMIE *watches him with a horrid fascination.*) Why, no, it's a policeman. It's Mrs. Bocking's brother.

(MUMMIE *draws her breath with horror and rushes from the room. Before this, however, and unseen by the audience, she must have managed to put the box with the brooch in her pocket.*)

(*Turning just in time to see her disappear through the door.*) Mummie! Where are you going? Mummie! Ts . . . ts . . . ts . . .

(*There is another knock on the door.*)

Well . . .

(*Looking rather annoyed he goes out to open the front door, and almost at once we hear voices in the hall.*)

Oh, it's you, Inspector. Come in.

INSPECTOR. Thank you, Mr. Sparkes. Lovely afternoon.

NELSON (*as they both come into the room*). Yes, isn't it? Excuse my hands. I've been gardening. Won't you sit down?

INSPECTOR. No, thank you. I only looked in for a minute or two. As a matter of fact, I've come to make you an apology.

NELSON. An apology? What for?

INSPECTOR. Well, I'm afraid my sister came in just now and rather upset your wife.

NELSON. Oh?

INSPECTOR. Yes. We had a burglary round here last night. You may have seen it in the papers. Lot of valuable jewellery stolen.

NELSON. Oh yes, I did see something about it.

INSPECTOR. Well, of course, Maude's got it on the brain. When I got home from the Yard just now she was full of a story of having seen an emerald brooch in your house, and as it just happens that an emerald brooch is the one piece of the stolen jewellery that we haven't recovered, I thought perhaps you'd let me have a look at it.

NELSON. Oh, certainly. But I don't think it can be the one you're looking for, because I bought it off a very nice man—a white Russian.

INSPECTOR. Really?

NELSON. Yes, you see his mother escaped from Petrograd in a silver aeroplane.

INSPECTOR. Did she? Well, if you'd just let me have a look.

NELSON. With pleasure. It was on the table. (*He looks about for it.*) Well now, where has it gone? Excuse me a minute. (*He opens the door and calls.*) Mummie! ... I expect my wife's taken it upstairs. Mummie! Will you bring down your new brooch, dear? The days do draw out, don't they, Inspector?

INSPECTOR. Where did you happen to meet this individual you bought the brooch from, Mr. Sparkes?

NELSON. He got into my carriage this morning.

INSPECTOR. Oh? What time was that?

NELSON. The eight-thirty-five. It was very empty this morning. We were the only two people in the carriage, and we got talking and he told me his story. It was most romantic. Oh, here you are, Mummie.

(MUMMIE *has come quietly into the room. All her fears seem to have vanished and she now faces* NELSON *and the* INSPECTOR *with a strange new calm.*)

INSPECTOR. Good afternoon, Mrs. Sparkes.

MUMMIE. What have you come for?

NELSON. He wants to see your new brooch, Mummie. There's nothing to be frightened of, dear. Have you got it?

MUMMIE. Yes. Here it is—in my blouse.

(*A jewelled brooch, which was certainly not there when she left the room, is pinned on her blouse.*)

NELSON (*looking at it*). No, dear. I said your *new* brooch.

MUMMIE (*determinedly*). This is my new brooch.

NELSON (*staring at her*). But, Mummie——

MUMMIE (*quickly—staring back at him*). This is my new brooch, Nelson.

INSPECTOR. But that isn't an emerald.

MUMMIE. No, it's a sapphire. It always was.

INSPECTOR. Ach! If that isn't just like Maude. She told me distinctly it was an emerald half-moon. You know, she gets so obsessed with every job I'm on that she sees clues everywhere. I'm so sorry for having bothered you. Good afternoon. (*He turns to go.*) Are your broad beans up yet?

NELSON (*proudly, going with him*). Up? We shall be eating them soon.

INSPECTOR (*as he goes out*). Can't understand it. I think the mice ate all mine. Pity you hadn't got the right brooch. There's a hundred pounds reward for it. We got the chap with all the rest of the stuff on him, but the best piece is missing. We think he must have dropped it. We shall find it, I expect. 'Afternoon, Mrs. Sparkes.

(*They disappear into the hall, and in a second the front door shuts. MUMMIE waits with trepidation for NELSON to come back, and never takes her eyes off the door. She is now over L., facing it.*)

NELSON (*coming back into the room*). Mummie! Whatever made you tell a police inspector a lie for? I'm not sure it isn't perjury.

MUMMIE (*crying copiously*). I did it to save you, ducksie.

NELSON. Save me? What from?

MUMMIE. The gallows.

NELSON. The gallows! Have you been out in the sun?

MUMMIE. You see, they said you were a murderer.

NELSON. Who did?

MUMMIE. Mrs. Bocking.

NELSON. Well, I never heard of anything so monstrous. Who'd I murdered?

MUMMIE. Mrs. Crawley. Mrs. Bocking said that was where you got the brooch. So when the policeman came I thought he'd come to arrest you and I—hid it.

NELSON. Where did you hide it?

MUMMIE (*crying*). In a dog.

NELSON (*sternly*). Mummie, do pull yourself together. In a what?

MUMMIE. A dog. I couldn't think of a safe place to hide it, so I wrapped it in a piece of meat—the piece you were going to have for supper—and gave it to a dog.

NELSON. But there's a hundred pounds reward for that brooch, Mummie. Which dog did you give it to?

MUMMIE (*wailing*). I don't know.

NELSON (*with great agitation*). Oh, come, you must know. There's a dog walking about somewhere with a hundred pounds inside it. I must buy it, you know. I must buy it. Whose dog was it?

MUMMIE. That's just it. It was a strange dog. I shouldn't know it again if I saw it.

NELSON (*almost violently*). Oh, Mummie! (*He subsides into a chair.*)

The CURTAIN *falls.*

MRS. CARTER*

CHARACTERS

Nelson Sparkes.
Mummie.
Sydney Carter.

When the Curtain *rises it is after dinner on an evening in Spring, and* Nelson *and* Mummie *are seated on either side of the fire—*Nelson *in his usual chair, up stage, and* Mummie *opposite him.*

Nelson *is wearing a black alpaca jacket with the trousers and waistcoat of his business suit.* Mummie *is in some dim dress. She is busy knitting.*

Mummie. Do you think we need the fire on to-night, ducksie?

Nelson. No, dear, I don't think so. It's quite warm.

Mummie. Where is it we're going to-night?

Nelson. Well, now, let's get the Bradshaw. (*He leans over to the rack by his side and takes out the Time Table.*) I thought we'd have a day on the Yorkshire Moors.

Mummie (*enthusiastically*). Oh yes!

Nelson (*turning over the pages*). Push on to the Lakes—that's a cross-country journey with a lot of changes: it ought to be most interesting. Then home by Wigan. We've never been to Wigan, have we, Mummie?

Mummie. No, dear.

Nelson. It'll make a nice round trip.

Mummie. You know, Nelson, I think I enjoy the journeys we take on paper much more than the real ones. It's so much more restful sitting here by the fireside than in a stuffy carriage—and we don't have to pack.

Nelson. Yes, I think the study of trains is most absorbing. I'd rather read my Bradshaw than any thriller you could give me. It's so exciting getting to a station and having only two minutes to catch the connection.

Mummie. Yes, and I think it's so clever of you, ducksie; because we've never missed a connection yet. You've got a wonderful head-piece for trains, I will say that.

Nelson. Yes, I flatter myself I know all the best trains to the principal towns in the country pretty well by heart. Now, are you ready? (*His finger is poised over a page of the Bradshaw.*)

Mummie. Yes, dear. Just a minute while I get my cushion

* Please see page 6.

B

straight. (*She pulls up the cushion a bit behind her back, and gives it a little pummel.*)

NELSON. We shall miss the train, you know, if you keep fidgeting. Now ... We catch the eight-thirty-five from here——

(*There is the sound of a dog howling mournfully outside.*)

MUMMIE (*looking up*). Oh, there's that dog again. I wish it wouldn't howl like that.

NELSON. Whose dog is it?

MUMMIE. The Carters'. I think it misses Mrs. Carter, poor thing. There's no one to take it out now she's away. Her husband doesn't take the slightest interest in it. Oh, by the by, he called here this afternoon.

NELSON. What for?

MUMMIE. Well, he wanted to know if I'd buy his wife's fur coat.

NELSON. What, the one she bought out of the money her aunt left her?

MUMMIE. Yes. I said it seemed a pity to sell it, but he said her sister's illness had cost such a lot of money.

NELSON. But Mrs. Carter's aunt left her three thousand pounds. It must be a pretty bad illness to cost all that. And why should *he* ask you to buy the coat? Why shouldn't Mrs. Carter write to you herself?

MUMMIE. D'you know, she's never written to me since she went. She never even answered that letter I wrote about the marmalade. I can't understand it.

NELSON. Are you sure you put the right address?

MUMMIE. I put the one she gave me—care of Mrs. Armitage, Langside, Gisborough, Yorkshire. That's her sister, Mrs. Armitage —the one who's ill.

NELSON (*thoughtfully*). How long has she been gone—Mrs. Carter?

MUMMIE. It must be quite six weeks. Yes, it was that bitterly cold Sunday, don't you remember? That's what makes it so funny about the coat. I mean, I can't think why she left it behind.

NELSON. It does seem funny. In fact, it seems very funny, I've thought so for a long time. (*Quietly, leaning forward in his chair.*) You know, Mummie, I don't think I like Carter.

MUMMIE. I don't think Mrs. Carter does, either. That's why I sometimes wonder if she'll ever come back.

NELSON. Yes. I've often wondered if—she'd ever come back.

MUMMIE. What do you mean, dear?

NELSON. Well, there's something funny about the way she went away. I thought so at the time. Why didn't she come and say good-bye to you? You're great friends.

MUMMIE. Mr. Carter said she hadn't time.

NELSON. Mr. Carter seems to have an answer for everything. It's funny she went away at night, too—and on a Sunday night. Trains are so much better on Monday morning. (*He gets up from his chair and begins to stroll thoughtfully to the french windows.*)

MUMMIE. Mr. Carter said the telegram from her sister only came at half-past eight, and it said "Come at once." So she went at once, you see.

NELSON. Did you ever hear her talk about her sister?

MUMMIE. Yes, but I had an idea she lived in Cornwall—not Yorkshire. 'Course, she may have moved. People do move, don't they?

NELSON (*by the window, looking out*). Yes, it looks as though Mr. Carter's going to move, too. There's a van outside the house now.

MUMMIE. That's the second van I've seen lately. What's he getting rid of now?

NELSON (*looking out*). They're carrying out the sofa from the front room.

MUMMIE. I wonder if he's moving up to Yorkshire to be near his wife?

NELSON. Whatever's that they're taking out now?

MUMMIE. Let me look, dear. (*She comes over to the window— stands looking out over his shoulder.*) There's something very heavy in that packing-case.

NELSON. Yes, the two of them can hardly carry it.

MUMMIE. I know. It's her books. Ducksie, you don't suppose Mr. Carter's selling his wife's things without her permission, do you? Because if so, I'd rather not buy that coat. (*She moves back to the fireplace.*)

NELSON (*also moving over*). It was rather an expensive one, wasn't it?

MUMMIE. Yes, it's a beauty. I've got it here. I must say, ducksie, it is a bargain. He only wants twenty pounds for it, and I'm sure it must have cost her eighty. It's a grey squirrel, you know, and they're not cheap.

NELSON (*still at the window*). Let's have a look at it.

MUMMIE. Yes; we shall have to make up our minds, because he said he'd come in this evening to see what I was going to do about it. It's in the hall cupboard. I'll fetch it.

(She goes into the hall.)

NELSON (*moving back to the table, reading the "Bradshaw"*). Gisborough . . . Yorkshire . . . Sunday trains . . .

MUMMIE (*coming back into the room—she is now wearing the fur coat*). Here it is. How do I look in it, ducksie?

NELSON. Oh, very rich. Very rich.

MUMMIE. It is my colour, isn't it? And it's so soft and so warm. Oh, if I had a coat like this I should never be parted from it.

NELSON. Exactly. I wonder why Mrs. Carter was?

MUMMIE. And it's quite perfect, you see.

NELSON (*pointing*). There's a little tear there by the pocket.

MUMMIE. Oh, that's only in the lining. (*She puts her hand in the pocket.*) Look. It would be easily mended. (*Suddenly.*) Oh!

NELSON. What is it?

MUMMIE (*her hand struggling in the pocket*). There's something in the lining here.

NELSON. Where?

MUMMIE. It's—it's paper, I think. Wait a minute. It's down between the lining and the fur. I've got it. Oh, it's a letter. (*She brings a crumpled letter from her pocket.*)

NELSON. Let me see.

MUMMIE. Oh, ducksie, ought you? It's a letter to Mrs. Carter. Look, it begins: "Darling Kathleen . . .!" That's her name, you know.

NELSON (*urgently*). Let me have it, Mummie. (*He takes it and looks at it carefully. A pause.*) It's signed, "Your loving sister." That would be Mrs. Armitage, I suppose?

MUMMIE. I suppose so. Though she always spoke of her as Violet.

NELSON. Well, but look at the address.

MUMMIE. Why, what is it, dear?

NELSON. Sea View Cottage, St. Ives, Cornwall.

MUMMIE. There! I said I thought she lived in Cornwall.

NELSON. And listen to this: "Edgar and I have taken on the cottage for another three months. It's heavenly here and I've never felt so well in my life. I was awfully disappointed at your letter saying you couldn't come down. I suppose Sydney's put his foot down as usual? Why ever don't you have the courage to leave him? We're both independent now—thanks to poor Aunt Ethel's money —and heaven knows you've put up with enough . . ."

MUMMIE (*a pause—then in an awed voice, looking at him*). Ducksie, what does that mean?

NELSON. It means that Mrs. Carter never went to stay with her sister.

MUMMIE. Then why did she go to Yorkshire?

NELSON. Perhaps she never did go.

MUMMIE. Yes, dear, but we know she went away that Sunday.

NELSON. Do we? We didn't see her go.

MUMMIE. But, dear, Mr. Carter *told* us she went away, and she certainly isn't here.

NELSON (*quietly*). No, I don't think she's here.

MUMMIE. Well then, where is she?

NELSON. That's what I'd like to know. Why did Mr. Carter say his wife's sister was ill? This letter's dated two days before Mrs. Carter's supposed to have left, and her sister was perfectly well then—she says so. Why did he say she was in Yorkshire, when she's living in Cornwall? Why is he getting rid of the furniture and trying to sell this fur coat? Why has Mrs. Carter never written to you? Mummie, I don't like this. I don't like it at all. There's something——

(The bell rings.)

MUMMIE. Oh, dear, I'm afraid that's him. He said he'd come about eight. Oh, you go, dear, will you? I don't like to. Wait a minute, though. What are we going to say to him, about the coat, I mean?

NELSON. Well, I think I'd like to ask him a few questions.

(He goes out of the room and we hear him opening the front door. In the meantime, MUMMIE *takes off the coat and throws it over the back of a chair. We now hear voices in the hall.)*

CARTER. Ah, good evening, Mr. Sparkes.

NELSON. Good evening. Come inside, won't you?

CARTER. Thank you. It's your good lady I want to see, really.

(He comes into the room, followed by NELSON. SYDNEY CARTER *is the kind of man one instinctively distrusts the moment one sees him. There is something shifty and uneasy in his manner which is somehow only emphasized by his extreme affableness. He is wearing a dark coat with a belt and has a tweed cap in his hand.)*

Good evening, Mrs. Sparkes. Ah, I see you've got the coat there. Have you made up your mind to have it? You won't regret it. It's a bargain.

NELSON *(suavely, shutting the door).* Sit down, Mr. Carter. I understand you're asking twenty pounds for the coat.

CARTER *(sitting in the chair above the fireplace).* Yes, and it's dirt cheap at the price. I'm sure you'll agree.

NELSON *(by his side—quietly).* Yes, why?

*(*MUMMIE *sits opposite him.* CARTER, *in the other chair, watches him closely.)*

CARTER. Eh? Why?

NELSON. Yes, why is it dirt cheap?

CARTER *(with forced jocularity).* Well, if that isn't looking a gift-horse in the mouth! That's all I get for making a special price to special friends.

NELSON. Mr. Carter. Am I right in saying that this coat was the property of your wife?

CARTER. Certainly it was—is.

NELSON. And was it bought with her own money?

CARTER. What's that to do with it?

NELSON. Only that I wondered if you had your wife's written authority to sell it.

CARTER. Well, what an insulting thing to say.

NELSON. I only wanted to be sure that your wife really *did* want to sell it. Winter's coming on and it's a beautiful coat.

CARTER. Well, of course she wants to sell it, or I shouldn't be offering it you. I had a letter from her only yesterday asking me to get rid of it and to give your wife the first refusal.

NELSON. That was from Yorkshire you had the letter?

CARTER. That's right. She's staying there with her sister, who's simply terribly ill. That's why my poor wife's got to sell her coat. Sister hasn't a bean, you know. We shall have to sell a lot more than the coat before we've finished, I can see.

NELSON. Yes, I see you're moving.

CARTER. Well, I'm just putting some of our stuff in store. As a matter of fact, I'm trying to get transferred to Yorkshire to be near my wife.

NELSON. Isn't she coming back again, then?

CARTER. I'm afraid she may have to stay up there indefinitely.

NELSON. Oh.

CARTER. You see, even if her sister gets over this, she'll be practically an invalid. Husband left her without a bean, you know. She's entirely dependent on us.

NELSON. Meanwhile it must be very awkward, you living here and your wife in—Gisborough.

CARTER. Yes, it is a bit. But it can't be helped at the moment.

NELSON. Who looks after you, then?

CARTER. No one. I look after myself.

MUMMIE. Don't you even have a woman in to do the house?

CARTER. I prefer being alone. You like the coat?

MUMMIE. Yes. Very much. It's so warm. I can't think why Mrs. Carter left it behind.

CARTER. Well, she had to go away in such a hurry, you know.

NELSON. You went with her, didn't you?

CARTER. Yes, poor thing, she was in such a state about her sister I couldn't let her go alone.

NELSON. No, no, of course not. I suppose you caught the night train from King's Cross—the twelve-fifteen?

CARTER. Yes, that's right. Beastly cold journey it was, too.

NELSON. I never could imagine how you got back to London so quickly on the Monday morning.

CARTER. But I didn't. I didn't get back till Monday afternoon.

NELSON. But surely I saw you going into a cleaner's in the Strand? You'd a parcel under your arm. I was interested because my hobby is trains and I couldn't think how you'd done it.

CARTER (*hardily*). You're mistaken. It wasn't me.

NELSON. Oh.

CARTER (*getting up*). I'm sorry, but I really must go now. And am I to leave the coat with you?

NELSON. No, I don't think so.

CARTER. What?

NELSON. I don't think we'd like to have it, thank you.

CARTER (*getting angry*). But you said just now—or Mrs. Sparkes did—that you were very keen on it.

NELSON. Oh, I think she's changed her mind, haven't you, Mummie?

MUMMIE (*timidly*). Have I, dear?

NELSON. Yes, I think so.

CARTER. What have you been wasting all this time for, then?

NELSON (*significantly*). Oh, I don't think we've been wasting time.

CARTER (*angrily*). D'you think I've nothing else to do than sit here listening while you twitter!

NELSON (*stung*). Twitter!

CARTER. Yes—twitter and yammer, all about nothing, when you didn't really mean to do business at all. Give me the coat! (MUMMIE *is about to hand it to him. He snatches it and makes for the door.*)

MUMMIE. Well, there's no need to snatch like that.

NELSON. And I shan't forget what you've said in a hurry, Mr. Carter.

CARTER (*at the door*). I hope you won't!

NELSON. Don't anger me, Mr. Carter. You may regret it.

CARTER. You futile little twirp.

(*He slams out of the room.*)

NELSON (*indignantly*). Twirp! Futile! The jackanapes! He deserves to be hu—— (*He suddenly realizes the implication.*) My word, I hardly know what he deserves.

MUMMIE. Ducksie, why did I have to change my mind about the coat?

NELSON. Have you ever heard of dead men's shoes?

MUMMIE (*horrified*). You don't mean Mrs. Carter's——?

NELSON. Well, where is she? She vanished on that Sunday night and nobody's heard of her since. Carter says he took her to Yorkshire. That was a lie, I know.

MUMMIE. How, dear?

NELSON. Because he said they travelled by the twelve-fifteen from King's Cross. Well, they couldn't have done because that train doesn't run on Sundays. There's no train out until five-thirty in the morning, and so he couldn't have got back on Monday by eleven o'clock when I saw him in the Strand.

MUMMIE. But why should he tell all these lies?

NELSON. Either Mrs. Carter ran away and he doesn't know where she is and doesn't like to say, or——

MUMMIE. Or what?

NELSON. Or she isn't anywhere, Mummie. I believe the poor woman's dead.

MUMMIE (*in an awed voice*). Nelson! You don't think he——?

NELSON. I'm afraid it looks very like it, dear.

MUMMIE. Oh no! How horrible. They didn't get on very well, I know; but surely he'd never——

NELSON. My dear, some men would do anything for money. And Mrs. Carter had just had three thousand pounds left her, and I know he's in debt to the tradespeople all round. If *she* wouldn't give him any of her money, he'd have a motive for getting rid of her—somehow. (*During this speech he has crossed to the french windows.*)

MUMMIE. What's the matter, dear? What are you looking at?

NELSON (*by the window—looking out*). That van's gone. Mummie . . . you know that packing-case they carried out. Did you notice how they carried it?

MUMMIE. Yes, dear. Two men had it on their shoulders.

NELSON. I know—like a coffin.

MUMMIE. No, no, I can't believe it! I can't believe anything like that of a person I've seen and spoken to, who actually lives opposite us.

NELSON. All murderers live opposite somebody, my dear, and are seen and spoken to by someone. Now, Mummie, we've got to do something. I'm sure he knew I suspected him. He'll be off to-night, I must ring up the police at once. (*He goes to the telephone on the table below the windows.*)

MUMMIE (*going to him*). Nelson, you can't! You haven't anything to go on. You don't really know anything. You only suspect. Suppose Mrs. Carter *did* have a sister called Mrs. Armitage and she *does* live in Gisborough, and she *has* gone there. We've never thought of that.

NELSON (*his hand on the receiver*). He still couldn't have got back from Yorkshire by eleven o'clock on Monday morning.

(The bell rings.)

MUMMIE. Oh! Supposing it's him come back. I'm frightened.

NELSON. Now, Mummie, we've got to keep our heads.

MUMMIE. But he may be armed.

NELSON (*calmly and bravely*). Give me the poker.

(MUMMIE *darts to the fireplace, grabs the poker and hands it to him.*)

MUMMIE. Oh, do be careful!

NELSON. Don't move while I go and answer the door.

(*With the poker grasped firmly in his hand and with a grim look on his face,* NELSON *marches slowly out of the room into the hall.* MUMMIE *stands watching him go, breathing heavily and twisting her hands. There is a tense pause.*)

MUMMIE. Well?

(*Then, a second later,* NELSON *returns, the poker hanging down by his side, and with an envelope in his hand which he is studying closely.*)

NELSON. It's all right. It was only the postman. It's a letter for you. Look at it. (*He hands it to* MUMMIE.)

MUMMIE (*taking it*). A returned letter. Now, who can that be from? (*She stares at it.*) Nelson!

NELSON (*returning the poker to the fireplace*). What is it?

MUMMIE. It's the letter I wrote to Mrs. Carter about the marmalade. You know—care of Mrs. Armitage, Gisborough. It says "Not Known."

NELSON (*grabbing the letter out of* MUMMIE'S *hands—staring at it*). Then there's no such person as Mrs. Armitage. (*Gravely.*) Mummie. There's no such person as Mrs. Carter either—*now*. (*He pushes past her.*) Out of the way, dear. (*He crosses quickly to the telephone.*)

MUMMIE. What are you going to do?

NELSON (*picking up the receiver—rattling the instrument*). Hullo? Hullo? Give me the Police, please. Yes, please—quickly! (*Under his breath.*) Twirp, indeed!

MUMMIE *stares at him bewilderedly and—*

The CURTAIN *falls.*

A NOD—A SNEEZE—AND A GOAT!*

CHARACTERS

NELSON SPARKES.
MUMMIE.
NURSE SCHOFIELD.
MRS. BOOKING.

When the CURTAIN *rises the clock on the mantelpiece is just striking seven o'clock.* MUMMIE *is seated in her usual chair by the fire, knitting. The door of the room is open. She looks up anxiously at the clock and as she does so the front door bangs.* MUMMIE *gives a little jump and nervously stows away her knitting in a bag.*

* Please see page 6.

MUMMIE (*calling*). Is that you, ducksie?

NELSON (*calling from the hall*). Yes, Mummie.

MUMMIE. Aren't you early to-night, dear?

(NELSON *comes into the room. He is wearing a dull-coloured suit, and a copy of the evening paper is tucked under his arm.*)

NELSON. No, dear. I opened the door on the third stroke of seven, as usual. Well . . . What have you been doing to-day?

MUMMIE (*awkwardly—trying not to look at him*). Oh—er—things, dear. Just things.

NELSON (*sitting down in his chair*). Did you go to the Jacksons' sale?

MUMMIE. The what, dear? The Jacksons'——? Oh yes. Yes, I did.

NELSON. Did you buy the lawn-mower?

MUMMIE. No, dear; it wasn't at all a nice lawn-mower.

NELSON. What was the matter with it?

MUMMIE. I don't know, dear. It wasn't a nice lawn-mower at all. I didn't buy it.

NELSON. Oh, well, that's saved the three pounds I gave you, hasn't it? (*Getting up.*)

MUMMIE. Er—— (*With a rush.*) Would you like your meal now, dear?

NELSON. No, I think I'll go and do half an hour's gardening first.

MUMMIE (*a shade desperately*). Oh, I shouldn't go out, dear—not in the garden. It's so—so draughty out there.

NELSON. Don't be silly, Mummie. It's a beautiful evening. Besides, you expect a draught outside. (*Suddenly.*) What's that noise, dear? (*There is a banging outside.*)

MUMMIE. Noise, dear? (*Quickly.*) Is there anything in the papers?

NELSON. About five sheets of news-print. *That* noise. That banging. It sounds as though it comes from the tool-shed.

MUMMIE. It's the oven door, dear—it flaps so. I'll go and shut it. (*She gets up and goes to the door which NELSON has shut on entering the room.*)

NELSON (*sniffing*). Are you cooking anything particular, Mummie? There's a funny smell.

MUMMIE (*at the door*). Smell, dear? Oh, that's onions.

NELSON (*sniffing harder*). No, it isn't. (*Another sniff.*) It's something nasty, Mummie. It's blowing in from the garden.

MUMMIE. I think it's the next-door's, dear.

NELSON. But surely, dear, they don't smell like that.

MUMMIE. No, dear, it's fish manure. They've put it on the garden.

NELSON. That's not fish. (*Sniffing again.*) Oh, Mummie, it's so strong.

MUMMIE. I'll shut the french windows, dear.

(*She goes across to the french windows, but before she quite reaches them there is a loud bleat from outside.* MUMMIE *stops dead in her tracks.*)

NELSON (*starting*). Mummie! What was that?
MUMMIE (*hurriedly and nervously*). I didn't hear anything, dear.

(*There is another loud bleat.*)

NELSON. There! It's an animal, Mummie. It sounds as if it's in the garden. It sounds like a sheep. It sounds like a *herd* of sheep. (*He rises from his chair.*) I'd better go and see.
MUMMIE (*guiltily—putting out her hand to stop him*). Nelson.
NELSON (*stopping before he gets to the window*). Yes, dear?
MUMMIE. That isn't a sheep. It's—it's—a goat.
NELSON. A goat? Whose goat, dear?
MUMMIE (*tearfully*). Our goat.
NELSON. Our goat? But we haven't got a goat.
MUMMIE (*more tearfully*). We have.
NELSON (*sharply*). Well, where'd we get it, Mummie? Come along. Where did we get it?
MUMMIE. I bought it.
NELSON. You—bought it! You bought a goat? Whatever for?
MUMMIE. Three pounds one and ninepence.
NELSON. But where? When?
MUMMIE. At the Jacksons' sale.
NELSON. But why? What do you want a goat for?
MUMMIE. I don't want it. I hate it. It's a beastly goat.
NELSON. Then what on earth made you buy it?
MUMMIE. My cold.
NELSON (*sternly*). Look here, Mummie, have you been taking something for that cold? Alcohol, I mean.
MUMMIE. No, dear. You see I was looking at the auctioneer and I felt I was going to sneeze—and just as he said "Any advance on three pounds?"—I went "Atishoo!" and he said "Thank you, madam"—and they gave me the goat. Nelson, you ought to have told me that if you sneezed at an auctioneer you'd bought a goat.
NELSON. Oh, Mummie, you must have nodded when you sneezed. He thought you were bidding. Oh dear, dear, dear . . . this is dreadful. I go up to town in the morning, all happy and unsuspecting, and come back to—to goats. It really is too bad of you, Mummie. You're not fit to be left. (*He goes to the window and looks out into the garden.*) Where is the thing? I don't see it in the garden.
MUMMIE. No, it's in the potting-shed.

Nelson (*turning on her—raising his voice in horror*). In the potting-shed—with my tomato plants? Mummie, really!

Mummie. Well, where *was* I to put it? I knew you wouldn't like it in the kitchen.

Nelson. I should think not. And what do goats eat? I suppose you didn't think to find *that* out?

Mummie. No. But I know now. They—they eat—tomato plants.

Nelson. What! Oh, this is awful. You don't mean to say it's eaten all my——?

Mummie. Yes, ducksie—every one—right down to the roots.

Nelson (*angrily*). That settles it. That goat goes right out of here first thing in the morning.

Mummie. But where? Where will it go?

Nelson. I don't care where it goes. I shall just open the shed door and shoo it out.

Mummie. I've done that once and a man brought it back—rather a fierce man, ducksie—and he made me give him five shillings.

Nelson. Well, Mummie, I can't say what I think of this and remain a gentleman. D'you realize we've only had that goat a few hours and already it's cost us three pounds five?

Mummie. Three pounds six and ninepence, dear—not counting the tomato plants.

Nelson. Be quiet!

Mummie. Don't be terse with me, ducksie. I'm so miserable.

Nelson. People who go about buying goats deserve to be miserable.

(*Fortunately for* Mummie *the door bell rings.*)

(*Irritatedly.*) Now, who's that?

Mummie. I can't see, dear. They're on the other side of the front door. Will you go, dear? I feel too upset to face anybody just now. Wait a minute till I've got into the kitchen.

(Mummie *goes hurriedly to the door and disappears, leaving it open.*)

Nelson (*following her out—muttering to himself*). Coming here and bothering people just when they're all messed up with goats.

(*The bell rings again just as he is going out.*)

All right, all right. . . . I'm coming . . .

(*A slight pause, then we hear voices in the hall.*)

Oh, good evening.

Nurse Schofield. Mr. Sparkes?

Nelson. Yes.

Nurse. Can I speak to you for a moment?

Nelson. Yes, come in. Will you go into the sitting-room?

(NURSE SCHOFIELD *strides into the room. She is the typical District Nurse: middle-aged, very matter-of-fact in her manner and obviously a person who stands no nonsense, either from her patients or anybody else. She wears the usual uniform and carries a bag.*)

NURSE. I shan't keep you a minute. My name's Schofield. I'm the District Nurse. Mr. Sparkes, is it true that you have a goat?

NELSON. Yes, I believe so. I haven't seen it yet. My wife only bought it this afternoon.

NURSE. Yes, I happened to hear by chance from someone who saw it in the garden. It seemed like Providence.

NELSON. What—the goat?

NURSE. Yes. You see, I have a patient—a little boy—for whom goat's milk is absolutely necessary, and as yours seems to be the only one in the neighbourhood, I thought perhaps you might be willing to sell it?

NELSON. Sell it? Oh. Oh, I see. But I'm not quite sure if this goat is the kind of goat that—er—provides milk.

NURSE (*bluntly*). I see. You don't know whether it's a nanny or not.

NELSON (*modestly*). No. But my wife would, I expect. I'll just call her and ask. (*Going to the door and calling.*) Mummie dear. Would you come here a minute? Providing our goat is—er—the right type of goat, did you—er—say you were thinking of buying it?

NURSE. Yes, my patients would. That's what I've come to see you about. What are you asking for the goat?

NELSON. Well, it's rather a special goat—an extremely active and healthy goat, I believe—and they're very difficult to find, as you know.

NURSE. Quite. But if you'd just tell me the price. I'm in rather a hurry.

NELSON. Well, a good goat runs at about six pounds now, you know.

NURSE. Well, we've got to have it—the little boy's very ill. But his parents aren't very well off. I don't think they could afford all that. You see, they gave me four pounds. They thought that would cover it.

NELSON. Oh. Oh, well, if the child's very ill you needn't give me four pounds. Give me three—or three-ten.

NURSE. Thank you very much. (*She opens her bag and takes out three pound-notes and one ten-shilling.*) Here are the notes . . . One. Two. Three—and ten shillings. (*She puts them down on the table in the centre of the room.*)

NELSON. Oh, but we haven't found out yet—Mummie!

MUMMIE (*appearing timidly at the door*). Yes, dear? Oh, good evening, Nurse.

NURSE. 'Evening, Mrs. Sparkes.

NELSON. Mummie dear, what—kind of a goat is ours?

MUMMIE. A black one, dear, with horns.

NELSON. That wasn't what I meant, dear. Is it?—has it?—can it——?

MUMMIE. Well, it can't do anything now, dear, because it's gone.

NURSE. Oh dear.

NELSON. Gone! But it can't have gone. I've just sold it.

MUMMIE. No, you can't have, dear, because it's gone. I've just let it out. It went rushing down the street bleating like anything.

NELSON (*sternly*). Mummie dear, you've no right to get rid of my goat like that. I'm very angry.

MUMMIE (*beginning to cry*). But, ducksie, you didn't want the goat. You said so.

NURSE. No, but I did, Mrs. Sparkes. Still, if it's gone, I suppose it's gone, and I'll have to try and get one somewhere else. Good evening. (*She turns towards the door.*)

NELSON. But wait a minute, Nurse. It can't have gone far. Mummie, you must go and find it.

MUMMIE. But where *shall* I find it, Ducksie?

NELSON. Well, look for it, dear. Look. You won't find the goat if you don't look.

NURSE. Well, I'm afraid I can't wait, Mr. Sparkes. I've heard of another one; it's ten miles off; but I must just get on my bicycle and go after it, that's all.

NELSON. Well, I'm very sorry. I'd have liked you to have had our goat.

MUMMIE (*fervently*). Oh, so would I!

NELSON. But, of course, we're still not sure, are we?

MUMMIE. What aren't we sure of, Nelson? You go on like this but you never tell me.

(*There is a ring at the bell.*)

NELSON. This house is like Clacton Pier on a Bank Holiday. Go and see who that is, Mummie, will you?

MUMMIE. Yes, dear.

(*She goes out, looking very crestfallen.*)

NURSE. Well, Mr. Sparkes, if you'll just give me my three pounds ten, I'll be off.

NELSON. I can only apologize, Nurse. My wife is a simple woman and is obviously unaware of a goat's—er—potentialities.

(*He is just on the point of picking up the notes from the table and handing them back to the NURSE, when there is a scream from the hall and the sound of MUMMIE's voice raised in angry protest, and a bleat.*)

MUMMIE. No, Mrs. Bocking! Not in the hall! I won't have it! I won't——! *OH!*

MRS. BOCKING'S VOICE. Yes, you will. It's yours and it's coming back where it belongs.

(*There is a noise of scuffling and bumping and banging.*)

NURSE. Whatever's that?

NELSON. It's our next-door neighbour, Mrs. Bocking.

NURSE. What—bleating?

NELSON. Excuse me, Nurse. (*Going to the door.*) What is it, Mummie?

MUMMIE (*in a distressed voice*). The goat, dear.

NELSON. Not in the hall!

MUMMIE. Yes. It's butted me. Oh, go away, you beastly thing. Go away!

(*There is a crash of china and the slam of a door.*)

Now look what it's done!

MRS. BOCKING (*coming into the room. She looks hot and ruffled and extremely angry*). It's nothing to what it's done to me. You should see my garden. It's disgraceful, Mr. Sparkes. People have no business to keep goats if they can't control them.

NELSON. Well, you see—it's rather difficult——

MRS. BOCKING (*in full spate*). D'you know what it's done? Put its feet through my frame——

NELSON. Oh dear, oh dear. . . .

MRS. BOCKING (*riding over him*). Stuck its beastly horn through the scullery window——

MUMMIE. Good gracious! Any bones broken?

MRS. BOCKING (*riding over her*). Trampled down my peas, ploughed up the lawn, and eaten a whole row of scarlet runners— *and* a vest of mine that was hanging on the line.

NURSE. The point is, did you notice the creature's sex?

MRS. BOCKING (*wildly*). Of course I didn't. A goat's a goat, isn't it? D'you suppose that when I saw it tearing up all my vegetables and eating my vest I could bother to think of a thing like sex?

NURSE (*with great dignity*). There's no need to be insulting.

MRS. BOCKING. And there's no need to be coarse either.

NELSON. Please, ladies . . .

NURSE. I never saw such a set of people. I'd better go and look for myself. Where is the thing?

MUMMIE. In the garden. She brought it in through the hall, ducksie, and it's smashed our china gnome.

NELSON (*touched to the quick*). Our china gnome, Mummie! How could you let it?

Mummie. I couldn't stop it, ducksie. It butted me. You see, Mrs. Bocking had got it into the kitchen by then.

Mrs. Bocking (*viciously*). Yes, and I hope it's eating *your* vegetables now—if it's got any appetite left.

Nurse (*indicating the french windows*). Excuse me, can I get out into the garden this way?

Nelson. Yes. Through the french windows. Shall I come with you?

Nurse. No, thank you. I don't think you'd be the slightest use. And I've left the money on the table.

(*She exits rapidly through the open french windows.*)

Mrs. Bocking. Look here, Mr. Sparkes, you and I'll have to have a talk about this. Your goat's done a lot of damage to my garden.

Nelson. But it isn't my goat.

Mrs. Bocking. Now don't you try that on with me. You know perfectly well it's your goat.

Nelson. It was, but I've just sold it. At least, I have if——

Mrs. Bocking. No "ifs" and "ands," please. Either that goat is yours or it isn't.

Nelson. Ah, but it isn't as simple as that, you see. It all depends——

Mrs. Bocking. It depends on what you're prepared to pay me whether I get my brother, the policeman, on to this or not.

Mummie. Oh, Mrs. Bocking. I'm sure Mr. Sparkes will do what's right. (*Aside to* Nelson.) After all, dear, we *are* being paid for the goat. You've got the money there. (*She points at the table.*)

Nelson (*aside*). Mummie, don't you understand? The goat may not be any use.

Mummie. Well, I knew it wasn't, dear, when I sneezed, but I couldn't help it.

Mrs. Bocking. I don't know what you're whispering about, but I want compensation, Mr. Sparkes. Seven-and-six for the frame, twenty-five shillings for the scullery window; we'll say a pound for the vegetables——

Nelson. Oh no, we won't—not your vegetables.

Mrs. Bocking. Yes, we will. Then there's four-and-six for my vest——

Mummie (*really roused*). No, Mrs. Bocking! That I cannot allow. If that vest fetched sixpence, I should be surprised. It was home-knitted in the first place—and very badly knitted at that.

Mrs. Bocking. How dare you say that my vest was badly knitted? After the socks I've seen on *your* line. Never does any pair have two feet the same length.

Nelson. Oh, please, please. . . .

MUMMIE. Be quiet, ducksie. Are you suggesting, Mrs. Bocking, that my husband's feet are malformed?

MRS. BOCKING. I don't know, thank goodness. But his socks are.

MUMMIE (*enraged*). You——! You——!

NELSON. Mummie dear, please don't sell her a youyou. I don't like language.

MRS. BOCKING (*stridently*). Mr. Sparkes, I'll take three pounds in full settlement.

MUMMIE. No, Nelson, don't give it her. Four-and-six for that vest is outrageous. Why, it's so thin with washing you can see through it. All their flannels are the same.

MRS. BOCKING. Will you kindly keep your tongue off my flannels.

NELSON. Really! Really!

MRS. BOCKING. Are you going to give me that money, Mr. Sparkes?

NELSON. Well, you see, my contention is that the goat—if it was sold—was sold before it damaged your garden.

MRS. BOCKING. I don't care when it was sold. It's done three pounds' worth of damage and I mean to get it back from somebody. If you say it's that nurse's goat, then I'll get it back from her. Where is she?

NELSON (*very awkwardly*). You see, Mrs. Bocking, we don't know till she comes back whether it *is* her goat or not.

MRS. BOCKING. Nonsense! It must be somebody's goat.

NELSON. The ownership of the goat, you see, Mrs. Bocking, rests on whether it's—well—masculine or feminine.

MRS. BOCKING. That's nothing to do with its appetite. It's eaten my vegetables and a valuable vest, and I demand compensation.

MUMMIE. And what about our gnome? If you hadn't brought the goat into the hall, our gnome wouldn't have been broken.

NELSON. Yes, it was a very valuable gnome. My wife was very fond of it.

MRS. BOCKING. Well, I didn't break the silly thing. It was your goat.

MUMMIE. Well, whose fault was it the goat was there?

NELSON. I think it's a nice point. Suppose we assume that our gnome cancels out Mrs. Bocking's vest?

MUMMIE. Never, ducksie! Never! Our beautiful gnome to be compared with a wretched threadbare vest.

MRS. BOCKING. Did you say threadbare?

MUMMIE. Yes, I did—*and* I meant it.

MRS. BOCKING (*threateningly—into* MUMMIE'S *face*). Just you say that again.

NELSON (*pleadingly*). No, don't, Mummie! Don't give in to her.

Mummie. Indeed I will. I'm not frightened of her. (*Hissing it back into* Mrs. Booking's *face.*) Threadbare! Threadbare! Threadbare!

(*Suddenly the* Nurse *pops her head in at the french windows.*)

Nurse. I say.

(*They all swing round to look at her and there is silence.*)

I'm afraid I must ask for my three pounds ten back. The goat's no good. It's a billy.

Quick Curtain.

NOTHING EVER HAPPENS *

CHARACTERS

Nelson Sparkes.
Mummie.
The Sailor.
Inspector.

When the Curtain *rises it is late on a summer evening, and* Nelson *and* Mummie *are sitting in their usual chairs on either side of the fireplace. The curtains over the french windows are drawn and the lights are, of course, lit. (An addition to the furniture in the room for this play, is a draught-screen in the* L. *corner, above the french windows.*)

Nelson *is wearing an old jacket with the dark waistcoat and trousers of his business suit, and on his feet are check carpet slippers.* Mummie *is in some sort of homely-looking dress with a woollen wrap round her shoulders, in a dull colour, which she has knitted herself. At first,* Nelson's *face is obscured by the evening paper which he is reading assiduously.* Mummie *is, as usual, knitting, with a pattern book laid out on the arm of her chair, which she consults from time to time. For a moment or two neither speaks.*

Mummie. Is there anything in the papers to-night, ducksie?
Nelson. Arsenal's won.
Mummie. Oh, that's nice. Won what, dear?
Nelson. Well, what d'you suppose they've won, Mummie?
Mummie. I don't know, dear. I'm asking you.
Nelson. Their match with Chelsea.
Mummie. Oh. I thought it was something real. Isn't there any news?

* Please see page 6.

NELSON. Well, they've found Mr. Martin and Miss Slazenger. Those people who were lost in the mountains.

MUMMIE. Oh, have they, ducksie? Where? Not—murdered, I hope?

NELSON. No, kidnapped by bandits.

MUMMIE. Oh, fancy.

NELSON. Yes, and it says here they were kept chained together for seventy-two hours before they were rescued.

MUMMIE. Oh, ducksie, and they weren't even married. What exciting lives some people do have.

NELSON (*reprovingly*). You're not hankering after that sort of excitement, I hope, Mummie. Not secretly wishing to be chained to Mr. Smith next door for seventy-two hours.

MUMMIE. Oh, ducksie, what a thing to say. What I meant was, we—we lead such quiet lives. Nothing ever happens to us.

NELSON. Well, what do you want to happen?

MUMMIE. Well, dear, there's a lantern lecture at the Parish Hall next Monday. It's called "A Trek Through Epping Forest." Couldn't we go to that? It *would* make a little excitement, and the tickets are only a shilling.

NELSON. Now, Mummie, we can't go throwing money away on treks through Epping Forest. What a craze for excitement you've got! Why, we went to the Ratepayers' Meeting only last week.

MUMMIE. Yes, I know, dear. I suppose I am a gad-about by nature.

NELSON. Besides, there's our summer holiday to think of. I've set my heart on being on the *front* at Bognor this year.

MUMMIE. Oh, ducksie, of course. That will be lovely. Instead of being opposite the gas-works like we've been the last two years.

NELSON. So just be patient and stop nattering about treks through Epping Forest and let me read my paper.

MUMMIE (*obediently*). Yes, dear. (*She consults the pattern book.*) Knit two together—three times—knit——

(*There is a loud banging on the front door.*)

Good gracious! Whoever's that? (*She tucks her knitting down at the side of her chair.*)

NELSON. You'll see when you've opened the door, dear, won't you?

(*Another bang.*)

MUMMIE (*getting up and going to the door*). Oh dear. It's someone in a hurry.

(*She goes out into the hall.*)

NELSON (*calling after her*). And ask them what they mean by trying to knock our front door in.

Mummie's Voice (*in the hall*). Oh! Oh, but you can't——You——! (*Shouting.*) Nelson!

(*The front door shuts with a bang.*)

Nelson (*getting up quickly*). What is it, Mummie?

(*He goes to the door and almost bangs into* The Sailor, *who comes quickly into the room at that moment. He is a young man with a racy manner and a sprightly imagination. His movements are all quick and impulsive; and all the time he is talking you can see he is listening and watching. He is wearing a rather shabby blue burberry coat and has a cap in his hand, which he soon puts down on the table in the centre of the room. His shoes are poor and dirty, and there is an air of raffishness about him. But he has a very pleasant smile and a twinkle in his eye.*)

Sailor. It's only me.

Mummie (*behind him*). Yes, ducksie, he pushed right past me. Most rude he was. I don't know who he is.

Sailor (*quickly*). You'll be very glad to see me when you know what I've come for. First of all, have I got the right people? What's your name, sir?

Nelson (*facing him*). Sparkes. Nelson Sparkes. But I——

Sailor. That's the name! I knew I was right. D'you know a Mr. Smith living in Afghanistan?

Nelson. No. No, I don't think so. Do we, Mummie?

Mummie. No, dear. Mr. Smith of Afghan—— No, dear.

Sailor. Well, he knows you.

Nelson. Dear me.

Sailor. I believe you once did him a very good turn, and he hasn't forgotten it.

Nelson. Did I? What did I do?

Sailor. Ah, that he didn't tell me. He didn't have time, poor chap. We were all among the sharks, see, and he was gone before he could do more than hand me his will.

Nelson. His will?

Sailor. Yes—a will in your favour, too.

Mummie (*with a gasp*). Oh, ducksie!

Sailor. I don't know how much it is. I don't like prying into other people's business, you know. But he was a rich man. I expect it's a tidy sum.

Nelson. Well, really, this has quite taken my breath away.

Sailor. Yes; doesn't happen every day of the week, does it?

Mummie. And I was just saying that very minute to Mr. Sparkes that nothing ever did happen.

SAILOR. Ah, you'll be able to go out and get yourself a couple of fur coats and a pair of snappy step-ins, eh, Ma?

MUMMIE (*shocked*). Well, really, ducksie. . . . (*She sits down in her chair.*)

NELSON. Am I to understand that this Mr. Smith gave you a will? Why did he give it to you?

SAILOR. Well, you see, guv'nor, our ship called in at Afghanistan last voyage——

MUMMIE. Oh, you're a sailor, are you? How——er——how breezy!

SAILOR. Yes, Ma.

MUMMIE. But you haven't got on sailor's clothes.

SAILOR (*jerking his thumb at* MUMMIE). 'Ark at 'er, guv. Can't get past Ma, can you? Knows what to look for in a sailor, eh? (*He chuckles hoarsely.*)

NELSON. You were saying you called in at Afghanistan?

SAILOR. Yes, for copra, you know. And I met this Mr. Smith, see? (*Listening.*) Did you hear anything?

NELSON. No.

SAILOR. Oh. Must have been my fancy.

NELSON. Well, you met this Mr. Smith?

SAILOR. 'Sright. And he took me out pearl-fishing with him, see? He'd just made his will that morning—he was telling me all about it, see, and how he'd left you all he had in gratitude for what you'd done, like.

NELSON. All?

SAILOR. Yes—every blinkin' penny.

MUMMIE. But—er—hadn't he a wife or anyone to leave it to?

SAILOR. Wife! That's just the trouble. He'd got three. All as black as your hat, too.

NELSON. Black? Dear me.

SAILOR. And he said to me as we were sitting in the boat, "If anything happens to me, Tinkles," he said—he always called me Tinkles, you know—my name's Tinkler—"if anything happens, don't let those three somethings"—pardon me French, Ma—— "or their sons get hold of my money. When you go back to England," he says, "you take my will to Lawyer Lightbody, him that lives in Piccadilly Circus, and he'll see old—er—what did you say your name was?

NELSON. Sparkes. Nelson Sparkes.

SAILOR. Ah, that's it. He'll see old Nellie Sparkes righted, he says. And they were the last words he ever did say.

NELSON. Dear me.

SAILOR. Yes, I told you we was out pearl-fishing, didn't I? Well, just then old Smith got a whoppin' great pearl on the end of his line.

MUMMIE. But I thought pearls came out of oysters.

SAILOR. Depends what sort of pearls, Ma. These were Afghanistan pearls. Black ones. The best in the market. Aren't they, guv'nor?

NELSON. I—er—really don't know. I don't know much about pearls. I'm in cheese, you know.

SAILOR. I see. Couple of cheese mites. Ha! Ha! Ha! (*His head on one side.*) I say, did you hear anything then?

MUMMIE. No. Do tell us what happened when Mr. Smith got the pearl on the end of his line.

SAILOR. Oh—what happened? Well . . . let's see. He was so excited pulling his pearl in, see, that he overbalanced and fell clean overboard. Next minute—click! A shark had his leg off.

MUMMIE. Oh, how dreadful.

SAILOR. I believe you. And of course once they've tasted blood—well . . . He'd only just time to 'and me the will out of what was left of his trouser pocket, before—click!—it 'ad the rest of 'im.

NELSON. What a most extraordinary story.

SAILOR. Yes, well, they always do say truth's stranger than fiction, don't they? Ah, well—that's that. Talkin's dry work, isn't it, guv'nor?

MUMMIE. Shall I make you some tea, Mr.—er——

SAILOR. Tinkler, Ma. You know—tinkle, tinkle, little star.

MUMMIE. Well, would you like some tea?

SAILOR (*confidentially*). Well, Ma, to tell you the truth, when you've been at sea as long as I 'ave, you find that tea 'aps to disagree with you. Something in the salt water, they say, rusts the gastric juices and nothing won't lay really 'appy, so to speak, 'cept spirits.

NELSON. Bring the flask, dear. You know where it is?

MUMMIE. Yes, dear, in the bottom drawer in the spare room under the blankets. We always keep a flask of alcohol, you know, in case of travelling, Mr.——

SAILOR. Ting-a-ling-a-ling!

MUMMIE. Oh yes—Tinkler. You are funny.

(MUMMIE vanishes, giggling.)

NELSON. Sit down, won't you?

SAILOR. Ta, very much.

(He sits down in NELSON'S chair, while NELSON sits opposite him in
MUMMIE'S.)

NELSON. Er—this will of Mr. Smith's. Where did you say it was?

SAILOR. At Lawyer Lightbody's. You know Lawyer Lightbody?

NELSON. I don't think I——

SAILOR. 'Course you do. Everyone knows Lawyer Lightbody.

Bang in the middle of Piccadilly Circus. I took the will there this morning as soon as I'd landed. Just a minute. (*The curtains over the french windows catch his eye.*) There's a crack in those window curtains. People might see in from the street, mightn't they? Would you mind pulling them?

NELSON. Yes, if you like.

(*He goes across to the curtains and is reaching up to pull them tight when* MUMMIE *comes in with a small tray with a flask, a glass and a jug of water.*)

MUMMIE. Don't touch the curtains, ducksie. One of those rings is none too safe. Here's the flask and a glass of water, Mr. Tinkler. I'm sorry we've no soda. Perhaps you'll help yourself. (*She stands by the chair, holding the tray out to him.*)

SAILOR. Water's stuff I never use, thank you, Ma. And what's the good of dirtying your glass?

(*He grabs the flask, holds it up a minute and says, "Well—here's mud in your eye, Ma!" then puts it to his lips, throws back his head and takes a deep drink, while* NELSON *on one side of him and* MUMMIE *on the other watch him fascinatedly.*)

MUMMIE (*as he gives her the toast*). Thank you, I'm sure. I hope you'll have mud in yours.

SAILOR (*wiping his mouth with the back of his hand*). That went down nice and easy. (*Suddenly.*) What's that noise? (*He grips the arms of the chair and listens.*)

NELSON. It's only someone walking by.

MUMMIE. You seem very nervy.

SAILOR. So would you if you'd been shipwrecked five times and had Beer and Skittles on your track.

(*He puts the flask back on the tray, which* MUMMIE *lays down on the table* O.)

MUMMIE. What on your track? I didn't quite catch.

SAILOR. Beer and Skittles. Cool! I haven't told you about them, 'ave I?

NELSON. Them?

SAILOR (*gravely*). Now, look here, you've got to be careful, guv'nor. They're after your money.

NELSON. Who are?

SAILOR. Beer and Skittles.

MUMMIE. You keep on saying Beer and Skittles, Mr. Tinkler. What *do* you mean?

SAILOR. They're old Smith's two sons—black as your boots, too. One's six foot four and the other's six four and a quarter. Woolly-haired, lips like lumps of steak and as naked as the day they were born—or they were before they came to England.

NELSON. You mean they're here—in this country?

SAILOR. Yes, they followed me all the way from Afghanistan, like a couple of cats after a poor little mousie. Wouldn't surprise me if they're in this street—perhaps looking in at this very window.

MUMMIE (*shuddering*). Pull the curtains tight, ducksie!

(NELSON *goes and gives the curtains a sharp tug.*)

SAILOR. Listen. Have you any children?

NELSON. No, alas. We have had hopes once or twice, but——

SAILOR. That's bad. You see, old Smith left it in his will that if you died without issue—that's kids—the money'd go to Beer and Skittles. And believe me, guv'nor, them two So-and-sos would stick at nothing to get it. Nothing.

NELSON. Oh, good gracious me!

SAILOR. Ah, and they're armed, too. Five bowie knives and a couple of ass-sissy-gayis they had when I last saw 'em. That's why I've got—this. (*He produces a revolver from his coat pocket for a moment.*)

MUMMIE (*with a frightened gasp, clutching at* NELSON). Oh, look, ducksie, he's got a pistol.

SAILOR. Now, what I've got to do is to disguise myself, see, so they won't know me when I leave this house. That suit you're wearing'll do, guv'nor. Might I trouble you to slip it off?

NELSON. What—me? This suit?

SAILOR. Yes, come on. No time to lose. You see, if I get out I can fetch the police and catch them before they do either you or Ma an injury. Sssh! Is that bare footsteps outside the window?

(MUMMIE *gives a little scream.*)

(*Roughly.*) Quiet! Now, come on, Dad. Off with the clobber.

NELSON. But really, I can't undress here in the sitting-room before Mrs. Sparkes and you.

SAILOR. We don't mind, do we, Ma? 'Sides, wouldn't you rather undress wherever it was than 'ave your 'ead sliced orf with an ass-sissy-gayi?

MUMMIE. Oh yes, do, ducksie. You can go behind the screen. We won't look.

NELSON. Well—really—this is most——

MUMMIE (*pushing him towards the screen*). Quick, dear.

NELSON (*muttering as he disappears behind the screen*). Very well. But, mind you, I don't like it . . .

SAILOR (*by the side of the screen*). Come on, quick! Let's have your coat and waistcoat. (*He thrusts his hand behind the screen and whips away the garments.*)

NELSON (*poking his head round the screen*). No, wait till I've taken my watch out.

SAILOR. Never mind your watch. The thing is for me to get the police before it's too late. You don't want them to come and find you in a pool of blood, do you? Now, your trousers.

(NELSON *throws his trousers over the top of the screen, muttering as he does so—"Oh dear, oh dear. . . ." The* SAILOR *catches them and puts them over his arm with the other clothes.*)

Here! Where are the braces?

(*He puts his hand behind the screen, grabs one end of the braces and pulls* NELSON *out with them, protesting violently.* NELSON *is discovered in a vest and long pants of wool of the shade called "natural." He looks very sheepish and cold.*)

(*Eyeing him over.*) Natty line in pants you're wearing, guv'nor.

NELSON (*shrinking back—determinedly*). No! There I do draw the line. You're not having those.

(*There is a ring at the bell.*)

MUMMIE. Oh! Oh dear, do you think it's those black men?

SAILOR (*alarmed*). I don't know who it is. Where does that door lead to on the other side of the hall?

NELSON. The kitchen.

SAILOR (*making for the door*). I'm going there to change my clothes. Wait till I'm there before you answer the door. And whoever it is—whoever it is, mind—I'm your nephew. Beer and Skittles may have put the police on to me.

(*The bell rings again.*)

(*At the door.*) Don't forget now—I'm your nephew.

(*He rushes out.*)

NELSON (*calling after him*). That's all very well, but how am I to explain why I'm like this?

SAILOR (*popping his head round the door*). Say you're practising yogi.

(*The bell rings again.*)

MUMMIE. I'm afraid to open it, ducksie. You go.

NELSON. What—like this? Don't be absurd, Mummie. Go along.

MUMMIE. But suppose it's Beer, or Skittles, or both?

NELSON. Here . . . take the poker. (*He darts over to the fireplace, gets the poker and hands it to* MUMMIE.) Don't keep them waiting any longer. You may make them savage.

MUMMIE (*groaning as she goes out to answer the door, the poker grasped menacingly in her hand*). Oh dear, oh dear, oh dear! ... Whatever's going to happen to us?

(*The moment she has disappeared,* NELSON *grabs the tongs and stands facing the open door, prepared for anything. Suddenly* MUMMIE *gives a faint shriek in the hall.* NELSON *jumps, and raises the tongs threateningly.*)

INSPECTOR's VOICE (*in the hall*). Good evening, Mrs. Sparkes.
MUMMIE. Goo-goo-good evening, Inspector.
INSPECTOR. May I come in? Thank you ...

(*The* INSPECTOR *comes briskly into the room.*)

(*As he comes in.*) Good evening, Mr. Spa—— (*He suddenly stops as he sees* NELSON *in his underclothes.*) Oh, I'm so sorry. Were you just going to bed?
NELSON. Oh no—no—no. I'm—er—(*quickly*) practising yogi. (*He sits suddenly cross-legged.*)
INSPECTOR. Really? A very interesting study, I believe. A bit chilly though, isn't it?
NELSON. No, no, I—I don't feel cold at all. Won't you sit down?
INSPECTOR. No, thank you. I haven't long to stay. *You* aren't going in for any of these fancy hobbies, are you, Mrs. Sparkes? I see *you* have the poker in your hand.
MUMMIE (*extremely flustered*). Oh—oh—er—I was just poking the fire, you see, when the bell rang.
INSPECTOR. Were you? What for? It isn't lit.
MUMMIE. Oh—oh—it was the kitchen fire. (*She takes the tongs from* NELSON *and puts them back in the fireplace together with the poker.*)
INSPECTOR. Ah, I see. (*Quite suddenly.*) Are you two alone to-night?
NELSON. Alone? W-why?
INSPECTOR. I was wondering whose cap this is. (*He picks up a cap from the table in the centre of the room; it is the one the* SAILOR *put down there when he came in.*)
MUMMIE. Oh—that's——

(NELSON *and* MUMMIE *exchange embarrassed looks.*)

INSPECTOR. Yes, Mrs. Sparkes?
NELSON. It's—er—it's our nephew's.
INSPECTOR. Oh? I didn't know you had a nephew.
MUMMIE. Oh yes, he's a sailor—from Afghanistan.
INSPECTOR. Funny place to be a sailor in, isn't it?
MUMMIE. You mean, because of the presence of sharks?

INSPECTOR. No, because of the absence of water.

NELSON. You know, it's been puzzling me all evening. I'm not very good at geography. Where is Afghanistan?

INSPECTOR. About the middle of Asia.

NELSON (*meaningly*). I see . . .

INSPECTOR. Where is your nephew, if I may ask?

MUMMIE. He's—er—in the kitchen.

INSPECTOR. I'd like to have a word with him. D'you mind if I—— (*He turns to the door.*)

NELSON (*hastily—getting between the* INSPECTOR *and the door*). Oh, I—I—I shouldn't disturb him, if I were you. He's—er—he's doing yogi, too. Only much more strenuously than me. He's—er—gone into a trance, I think.

MUMMIE. Oh, Inspector, do you mind my asking, has your coming here anything to do with—Beer and Skittles?

INSPECTOR (*bewildered*). Beer and Skittles, Mrs. Sparkes?

(*There is suddenly a confused noise of shouting and scuffling outside, and a revolver shot.*)

My God! He's shooting. Let me get past, Mrs. Sparkes.

(*He dashes past* NELSON, *nearly knocking him over, and out through the door.*)

MUMMIE. Ducksie, did you hear? That was a shot.

NELSON. Lie down, Mummie! On your face. They may shoot again.

(*They both crouch down side by side, flat on the floor.*)

MUMMIE. I suppose it's Beer and Skittles. D'you think they've shot him, poor fellow?

NELSON. I don't know *what* to think, Mummie. In fact, I find it difficult to think at all without my clothes.

MUMMIE. Hadn't I better go and see if Mr. Tinkler's still in the kitchen?

NELSON. Stay where you are. I'll call. (*Poking his head above the seat of the chair—calling.*) Er—I say, Tinkler! Are you all right? (*A pause.*) He doesn't seem to answer, Mummie.

MUMMIE. Oh, ducksie, perhaps he's lying dead. Shot by those awful black men, trying to protect us. How noble.

(*The* INSPECTOR *strides into the room, sees it empty; turns to the door and calls out.*)

INSPECTOR. Mr. Sparkes! Mr. Sparkes, where are you?

NELSON (*getting up from the floor*). We were just lying on the floor for a rest.

MUMMIE (*following his example*). Yes, we do sometimes, you know.

INSPECTOR (*seeing them now*). Well, you can get up now. There's no more danger. We've got your nephew from Afghanistan—or rather Joe Simpson.

NELSON. You've got him? What for?

INSPECTOR. Burglary. He's just broken into a house in this neighbourhood. We've been after him the whole evening. Desperate character, too. You had a narrow escape. You know, you might have got yourselves into serious trouble hiding a man like that. What made you do it? If I hadn't been a friend of yours, you'd have been had up for harbouring a criminal.

MUMMIE. But we didn't *know* he was a criminal. Did we, ducksie? He said he'd come to tell us—oh, Nelson—the will!

NELSON. I'm afraid, Mummie, that there isn't any will.

INSPECTOR. Did he take anything of yours?

NELSON. Well, there's my suit. He was probably wearing that.

INSPECTOR. I see. So *that's* why you were—er—practising yogi, Mr. Sparkes.

NELSON (*rather ashamed of himself*). He tells a remarkably convincing story, Inspector.

INSPECTOR. It's part of his stock-in-trade. Anything else beside the suit?

NELSON. I don't——

MUMMIE. There was your watch, ducksie—in the waistcoat pocket.

NELSON. Oh yes.

INSPECTOR. I'll send a man round with those from the station. I must be off to charge Simpson. I'll say good night.

NELSON }
MUMMIE } (*together*).   Good night.

(*The* INSPECTOR *goes out, shutting the door and then the front door.*)

MUMMIE. Oh, ducksie, I feel quite faint. (*She drops into her chair.*)

NELSON (*wagging his finger at her*). Well, let that be a lesson, Mummie. Look where your craving for excitement's led us. We've lost a big legacy—not that I really ever believed in it—and my suit's probably got a bullet through it, and——

MUMMIE. Yes, ducksie, but we've lost Beer and Skittles, too—and that's a relief.

NELSON. Well, now I hope you'll settle down and be quiet.

MUMMIE. Oh yes, ducksie. I've had quite enough agitation. I don't think I even want to go that trek through Epping Forest now.

The CURTAIN *falls.*

CREAM OF TARTAR *

CHARACTERS

NELSON SPARKES.
MUMMIE.
AUNT REBECCA.
SHARPE.

When the CURTAIN *rises it is a Summer evening and* MUMMIE *is just putting a cushion on* NELSON'S *chair, which she pats into a comfortable angle. As she does so,* NELSON *walks in. He has just got home and is in his usual business suit, with the evening paper under his arm.*

NELSON. I'm home, Mummie.

MUMMIE *(a little faintly)*. Oh yes, dear. So you are.

NELSON. Is the meal ready?

MUMMIE. Well, dear, I thought we wouldn't have it yet. We'd have it about nine—a sort of supper.

NELSON. But why? I want to get out into the garden.

MUMMIE. Yes, dear, I know. So I thought to myself, Ducksie can have a nice long time in the garden while it's light—so as not to waste the daylight, you see—and then he can come in about nine, all ready and eager for the meal. It'd be a nice change.

NELSON. I don't like change, Mummie. You know I don't. It upsets me. I wish you wouldn't do these things. Besides, I'm hungry. *(He slumps down into his chair, looking very annoyed.)*

MUMMIE. Well, dear, would you like a nice piece of seedy cake? I made a lovely one this morning.

NELSON *(severely)*. Mummie. When a man's inside is crying out for fish and chips, or bacon and eggs, it's no good offering him cake. I know you mean well, but you've spoilt my day.

MUMMIE *(sitting down dejectedly in her chair)*. Oh, ducksie, I am sorry. But don't you think, living as we do, just the two of us, we're apt to get into grooves?

NELSON. I like grooves. You know where you are with grooves. They're comfortable: they're safe: you can see where they lead to. I hate surprises. No, Mummie, don't keep waving that cake in front of me. I don't *want* it. *(Sufferingly.)* I shall wait till nine. I shan't enjoy my gardening. I can't work on an empty stomach—you know that quite well. But what do you care? Nothing!

MUMMIE. Oh, ducksie, you *are* cross.

* Please see page 6.

NELSON. I'm not cross at all. But when you deprive a hungry man of food, Mummie, you do a serious thing, and many a marriage has come to grief because of it.

MUMMIE. Oh, Nelson, don't make things more difficult for me to-day. I've—I've got something to tell you.

NELSON. Don't say you've bought another goat, Mummie; because if so, I shall lose my temper.

MUMMIE. I haven't bought anything, ducksie; but it's nearly as bad.

NELSON. What's nearly as bad?

MUMMIE. What's happened.

NELSON. Well, what *has* happened? (*Sternly.*) Mummie! You've smashed my Coronation shaving mug.

MUMMIE. No, ducksie. No. I almost wish I had.

NELSON (*aghast*). *What!*

MUMMIE. I mean—I wish it *was* only that.

NELSON (*impatiently*). Well, come along now, Mummie. Come along. What is it?

MUMMIE (*faintly*). It's—it's Aunt Rebecca.

NELSON. Well, what's the matter with the silly old woman?

MUMMIE. Nothing. She's here.

NELSON. Here?

MUMMIE. Yes. At least, she's gone out at the moment to buy some birdseed. That's why we can't have the meal till nine. (*There is an awful pause.*) Ducksie, say something.

NELSON. I can't, Mummie. I'm afraid to speak. (*He gets up and paces about the room.*)

MUMMIE. I thought you'd take it like this, ducksie. I know you've never been very fond of Aunt Rebecca.

NELSON (*almost screaming*). Fond! Fond! *What* an under-statement! Can one feel fondness for a viper, Mummie? Can one cherish a snake? Can one have any affection for a hedgehog?

MUMMIE. Oh, ducksie, I don't think you ought to call Aunt Rebecca all those things.

NELSON. Yes, and there are a lot more things I could call her, things beginning with a B, only I'm so angry I can't think of them. Why didn't you tell me she was coming?

MUMMIE. But, ducksie, I couldn't tell you she was coming. I didn't know. The bell rang and I went to the door and there she was with four trunks, a basket chair and a canary.

NELSON. Four trunks! Then she's going to stay. Mummie, don't say it's for good, or I shall go. I couldn't stand it. I should go mad.

MUMMIE. Well, dear, she said she couldn't stay where she was: they were stealing from her.

NELSON. Were they? Were they, indeed? They were clever

people. I should like to meet them. To get anything from that mean, grasping, suspicious, miserly old hag—yes, hag, Mummie—hag, hag, hag——

MUMMIE. All right, dear, I heard.

NELSON. Well, it was something of an achievement. We've never even had a twopenny bus fare out of her all the times she's stayed with us.

MUMMIE. I wouldn't mind bus fares so much, ducksie; but when it comes to seven-and-six for a taxi——

NELSON (glaring at her). Seven-and-six! *You* paid seven-and-six? Mummie, I shall have a fit—a gasping, choking fit. I shall never be civil to her. Every time I look at her I shall think seven-and-six, and I don't know what'll come out of my mouth.

MUMMIE. Oh, please, ducksie—just for my sake. She *is* my aunt, you know; and we're all she has to leave her little bit of money to.

NELSON. Yes, I know. She'll stay here for years, take everything she can get, have a long and expensive illness, and then leave everything to a Home for Crippled Canaries. It's too much, Mummie! It's too much!

MUMMIE. Well, ducksie, I really think she's trying to be nice this time.

NELSON. Nice! That's a word she's never heard of, Mummie.

MUMMIE. Well, she's been doing ever such a lot of gardening for you this afternoon.

NELSON (with a strangled cry of anguish). Gardening! What has she done? Tell me quickly, Mummie. Where has she been gardening?

MUMMIE. Well, dear, she's been very kind, really. She brought a packet of some absolutely new kind of bean that we've never heard of before—she says they taste something between peas and asparagus and crop all the winter. She's planted a whole row.

NELSON. But how could she? The garden's full. Where's she put them? Mummie, if *she's* dug up the grass——

MUMMIE. Oh no, dear. No, she's done nothing like that. She just had to—to move those scarlet runners.

NELSON. Move! Move my scarlet runners when they're just up and ready for sticking! The woman's not fit to live, Mummie. A person who'll interfere with a man's scarlet runners is capable of anything. I mean, it hits a man in his tenderest place, that does, Mummie. You'd no business to let her.

MUMMIE. But I couldn't stop her. And after all, when we get the new beans——

NELSON. We never shall. And why? Because I'm going down now to stamp on her wretched beans. Stamp on them—with both feet, Mummie.

(*He marches towards the french windows, but suddenly stops as the bell rings.*)

(*Turning round to* MUMMIE). Who's that? I suppose it's your Uncle Frank come now with his six children. Or perhaps your Auntie May with her two asthmatic spaniels.

MUMMIE (*getting up to go to the door*). Oh, ducksie, don't go on.

NELSON. Oh no! I'm not to say a word. My wife can *fill* the house with her relations, all grubbing up my vegetables and trompling over my garden, and I'm not to say a word.

MUMMIE. But I haven't got all my relations, ducksie. Only Aunt Rebecca.

(*The bell rings again.*)

NELSON. The rest are probably waiting outside. Go and open the door.

MUMMIE (*as she goes out*). Oh dear, oh dear, everything's going wrong to-day . . .

NELSON (*muttering to himself*). Wretched old woman . . . I'll give her beans . . .

(*We hear* MUMMIE *opening the front door and voices in the hall.*)

MUMMIE. Oh! Oh, good evening.

A MAN'S VOICE. Good evening, Mrs. Sparkes. Could I have a word with you?

MUMMIE. Certainly. Will you come in?

(SHARPE *comes into the room, followed by* MUMMIE. *He is a serious-looking young man with a polite manner. At the moment he is more serious than usual.*)

Oh, this is my husband. Oh, ducksie, this is the young man from the chemist!

NELSON. Has he come to stay, too?

MUMMIE (*reprovingly*). Ducksie!

NELSON. Well, everybody is.

SHARPE. Sorry to bother you, sir. My name's Sharpe, by the way. But I sold you a packet of cream of tartar this morning, Mrs. Sparkes, didn't I?

MUMMIE. Yes. Yes, you did.

SHARPE. Well, do you think I could have it back?

MUMMIE. You can have some of it back, but not all.

SHARPE. Good lord! You haven't used it, Mrs. Sparkes?

MUMMIE. Of course I have. I made a cake—a lovely cake, too. Why?

SHARPE. Oh, my goodness. You haven't eaten any of it, have you—the cake, I mean?

MUMMIE. No, but my aunt has. She had ever such a large slice for her tea and remarked what a good cake it was. Have you run short of cream of tartar, then?

SHARPE. Mrs. Sparkes, I don't want to alarm you, but—that—wasn't cream of tartar you had.

MUMMIE. Wasn't it?

SHARPE. No. As a matter of fact, there's been a ghastly mistake. There were three packets on the counter this morning: two were cream of tartar and the third was a packet of a new preparation of arsenic that we'd just had delivered from the wholesalers. We've got *one* packet of cream of tartar, but the arsenic's gone. I've only just found it out. I came round at once.

NELSON. Good heavens!

SHARPE. You said your aunt ate some of the cake. Is she still—all right?

MUMMIE. She was a little while ago.

NELSON (*bitterly*). She was well enough to do some *gardening*.

SHARPE. Well, of course, the action of the poison is sometimes delayed, but never for very long, as a rule.

MUMMIE. What will it—do to Auntie?

SHARPE. Well, it's pretty serious. It may kill her, Mrs. Sparkes.

MUMMIE (*with a gasp*). Oh no!

SHARPE. Well, it may. Where is she?

MUMMIE. She's out. Gone to buy seed for her canary.

NELSON. Oh, how careless of you, Mummie, to let her go out after arsenic. She may be lying groaning now in the birdseed shop.

MUMMIE. Well, ducksie, how did I know I'd given her arsenic? Oh dear, what are we to do now?

SHARPE. Have you got the rest of the packet?

MUMMIE. Oh no, I forgot. You see, Mrs. Bocking from next door came in to borrow some and I said "Help yourself, Mrs. Bocking," I said—and she did. She took the packet.

SHARPE. Oh, my goodness! D'you think she's used it?

MUMMIE. Yes, because she said she was going to make soda scones for the children's tea.

SHARPE. Children? How many children?

NELSON. Six.

SHARPE. My God! I must go. (*He turns quickly to the door.*)

NELSON. But you can't. You can't go like that.

SHARPE. But I must. Think of those six children!

NELSON. Well, think of our aunt. She's an old lady. What are we to do with her?

SHARPE (*at the door*). Give her an emetic.

NELSON. What emetic?

Sharpe (*as he goes out*). Salt and water. Make her drink as much as she can.

(*The door bangs after him.*)

Nelson. Well, *there's* a nice thing you've done, Mummie. You look like being had up for auntiecide.

Mummie. What's that, ducksie?

Nelson. Aunt-murder.

Mummie. Oh, don't, ducksie! Don't say that—even in fun.

Nelson. There's no fun about this, Mummie. It's deadly serious. If that aunt of yours dies, we may be had up for murder. There's a motive, you know. We're her only relations, and she's got a bit of money.

Mummie. But you don't mean to say anyone would think that I —that we——

Nelson. Leave me out of it. I didn't make the cake.

Mummie. No, but everybody knows you didn't like poor Aunt Rebecca. You said so the other night in front of Mrs. Bocking. What'll *she* think?

Nelson. She won't have time to think with six children suffering from arsenical poisoning.

Mummie (*crying*). Oh, ducksie, I wish you wouldn't. (*She sits down in her chair.*)

Nelson. Well, we've got to face facts.

Mummie. I wish Auntie would come home.

Nelson. She won't be able to come. She'll be brought.

Mummie. Poor Aunt Rebecca, I can't bear to think of it. What had she ever done to anyone?

Nelson. Done! She'd pulled up my scarlet runners. It only shows you, Mummie, how quickly your sins find you out.

Mummie (*gripping the arm of her chair*). Hark! Was that a groan?

Nelson (*in an awed voice—looking towards the door*). Yes. It was.

Mummie. D'you think it's her?

Nelson. I'm afraid so. Now we must keep our heads, Mummie. We mustn't alarm her. You go into the kitchen and get a good big glass of salt and water. We must try and get her to drink it.

Mummie (*getting up*). Supposing she won't? It can't be very nice.

Nelson. We must disguise it somehow. Now, don't make difficulties, Mummie. We've *got* to get it down her.

(*The groans are now audible, getting nearer.*)

Quick, before she comes in!

(Mummie *rushes to the door and nearly knocks* Aunt Rebecca *down, for she just comes into the room at that moment.*

*She is a grim old lady with a harsh, rasping voice and a quelling
eye. She walks rather unsteadily, with a sort of hobble, and stoops a
little. She is wearing a black coat and a black hat with lace and a
feather boa that has seen better days. She looks hot and ruffled, and
out of temper and groans; and every time she groans her hand flies to
her back.)*

AUNTIE (*groaning*). Oh! Oh!

NELSON (*sweetly*). Hullo, Auntie dear. How are you? Pretty
well?

AUNTIE. No. I'm neither pretty nor well. I'm upset.

NELSON. Oh, are you? Sit down in the armchair. (*He places*
MUMMIE'S *chair invitingly for her.*)

MUMMIE. And I'll go and get you a nice drink of water. You look
done up.

AUNTIE (*hobbling across to the chair*). That's a pretty thing to offer
anybody, that is. Water. Oh! (*She groans.*)

NELSON (*playfully*). I know. I know the very thing when you're
feeling like that. A teaspoonful of salt in the water. Picks you up no
end. Get her some salt and water, Mummie.

AUNTIE (*lowering herself gingerly into the chair*). Don't you dare.
Salt and water, indeed. What d'you take me for—a whale? Oooh!
I done too much gardening, that's what it is.

NELSON (*at the back of* AUNTIE'S *chair—aside to* MUMMIE). We shall
have to try mustard if she won't take salt.

MUMMIE (*under her breath*). Plain mustard, ducksie?

(*They are now both well down stage, behind* AUNTIE.)

NELSON. Of course not. We must put it in something. Have we
got any beer?

MUMMIE. There's half a bottle left over from your birthday last
month.

NELSON. That'll do. Put it in that. A good heaped teaspoonful
of mustard. I should put the salt in too to be quite safe. Hurry up.
She's looking a bit blue. There's no time to lose.

MUMMIE. I'll go now.

(*She goes out.*)

AUNTIE (*turning round in her chair*). What are you whispering
about, you two? Here am I groaning in pain, and all you can do is
to stand in the corner of the room and whisper. Can't you *do*
anything for me? Oooh! I wish I hadn't stooped.

NELSON. Well, Auntie dear, as a matter of fact, that's what
Mummie and I were talking about. We've got the very thing for
you. A special bottle of wine.

AUNTIE. Wine? What's it like?

NELSON. Well—it's—as a matter of fact—it's an old Indian remedy given to me by a Choctaw chief who comes into the office sometimes to buy cheese. He says it'll cure anything from warts to housemaid's knee.

AUNTIE. But I haven't got either, you silly man.

NELSON. No, that's why it'll cure you. (*Calling.*) Got that stuff, Mummie?

MUMMIE (*calling back*). Coming, dear.

NELSON. Are you quite comfortable, Auntie dear? Have this footstool for your feet. . . . And now a cushion. . . . That's right.

AUNTIE. Very affable all of a sudden, aren't you? What's the matter? Want to borrow some money?

NELSON. Oh, Auntie, that *is* unkind. I'm just very very sorry you're not feeling well. Ah! Here's Mummie with the wine.

(MUMMIE *comes in with a glass of a peculiar-coloured liquid which she offers to* AUNTIE.)

Now, Auntie, you've got to throw your head back and drink it all down at a gulp, otherwise it won't do you any good.

AUNTIE (*making no effort to take the glass*). I'm not drinking anything down at a gulp until I've tasted it first. Many an old woman with money has done that and never lived to regret it. Oooh! (*She groans.*)

NELSON (*aside to* MUMMIE). She's getting worse. We've got to get this down her somehow. Now, Auntie, come on. Be a good girl and drink this for Nelson.

AUNTIE (*fixing them both with her eye*). Here, why are you so anxious for me to drink that? What is it?

MUMMIE. Oh—it's—it's an old Spanish recipe, Auntie. A cure for heartburn. Nelson dear, do get off my foot.

(NELSON, *in a frantic endeavour to stop her talking, has trodden on her toe.*)

AUNTIE. Here, I don't like this.

MUMMIE. You will when you drink it, Auntie. You'll love it. It's got such a bite. (*She holds out the glass for* AUNTIE *to take.*)

NELSON. Now, come on. Shall I hold your nose?

AUNTIE. No, you will not! You leave my nose alone.

NELSON. Now, please, Auntie dear, don't be difficult. We're only trying to help you.

AUNTIE. I don't believe you are. I believe you're trying to do something else to me. I believe you're trying to *poison* me.

NELSON (*bravely*). Poison you, Auntie? Ha, ha, ha! *What* an idea.

AUNTIE. Yes, it *is* an idea. It's my idea. Here, Nelson, you have a drink of this first.

NELSON. Oh, thank you very much, Auntie. I should love to, but it's all we have left, and *you're* the one who *really* needs it. Come on. You drink it up.

AUNTIE. Not a sip till I see one of you taste it first.

NELSON. Oh, very well. Mummie—humour Auntie, dear. Drink a sip of it just to show her.

MUMMIE. Oh—er—it would get into my head, dear. You've a *much* stronger head. You drink it. (*She holds it out for* NELSON.)

AUNTIE. Just as I thought. You daren't drink it—either of you. Oh! Oh! I'm alone with you. I'm alone with a couple of murderers. (*Shouting.*) Help! Help! (*She sways about in her chair.*)

NELSON (*clapping his hands at her*). Auntie! Auntie, be quiet! For goodness' sake. The neighbours'll hear you.

AUNTIE. I want them to hear. Help! Hel——!

(*She begins to gobble as* NELSON *holds his hand over her mouth.*)

MUMMIE. Oh, Nelson, be careful! You may knock her teeth down her throat.

(AUNTIE *gobbles frantically behind* NELSON'S *hand, and wriggles to get free.*)

SHARPE (*rushing in—panting*). Excuse me coming in like this, but the door was open. I just came to tell you it's all right. It's all right.

AUNTIE. What's all right?

SHARPE. You. You're not poisoned.

AUNTIE. Well, I know that, you silly noodle. But I very nearly was. If you hadn't come in when you did you'd have found me asphisticated by these murdering Sparkeses.

NELSON. D'you mean to say it wasn't—er—what we thought it was in the cake?

SHARPE. No. I've just been down to the shop. The other packet—the deadly one—has been found. Sorry to have caused all this bother. I must tell the Bockings, too. Good night.

NELSON. Good night.

(SHARPE *goes out and we hear the bang of the front door.*)

AUNTIE. So I was right. You wicked, murdering frights. You *did* mean to put something in my food—something deadly, he said—but he gave you the wrong packet, did he?

MUMMIE. Auntie! Auntie! You don't understand.

AUNTIE. I understand all I want to. I don't blame you so much. You're a catspaw. It's him that's the villain. Wanted to get rid of me, did he? Well, he's done that all right. *I'll* never darken his wicked doors again, and I'll strike his murdering name out of my will. Where's my hat? (*She picks it up from the floor by her side and begins to hobble to the door.*)

MUMMIE. Where are you going, Auntie?

AUNTIE. Out of this house!

(*She slams out of the room.*)

MUMMIE. Oh, ducksie, now she won't leave us any money.

NELSON (*feelingly*). No. But she'll leave us alone.

Quick CURTAIN.

SPIES IN THE CELLAR*

CHARACTERS

NELSON SPARKES.
MUMMIE.
MRS. BOOKING.
ALICE.

It is an Autumn evening and the curtains are drawn over the french windows in MR. *and* MRS. SPARKES'S *little sitting-room. A cosy fire is burning in the grate and* NELSON *and* MUMMIE *are sitting on either side of it enjoying the warmth.* MUMMIE *is knitting as usual and ready with a bright comment on any item of news* NELSON *may read out to her from his evening paper.*

An addition to the furniture of the room for this play is an old walnut bureau which should be against the R. *wall, down stage, below the french windows, in place of the small table and telephone.*

NELSON. It's a bit chilly to-night, Mummie.

MUMMIE. Is it, dear? I'm afraid there's no more coal in the scuttle. I'll get some. (*She rises eagerly.*)

NELSON. Sit down, Mummie. I'm not going to have you hauling coal-scuttles about. What's Alice for?

MUMMIE (*rather scathingly—sitting down again*). Ornament, I should think, dear—for all the work she does.

NELSON. You won't *let* her do any work. You do it all yourself.

MUMMIE. Well, I always have done the work myself all the years we've been married. I never wanted a maid, and if I had wanted one, it wouldn't have been Alice.

NELSON. Of course you took a dislike to her the moment she came in. Just because *I* engaged her.

* Please see page 6.

MUMMIE. Well, why *did* you engage her? You never said anything to me—never even asked me. Just came home one night and informed me that Alice was arriving next day. I had to sit up half the night cleaning the house ready for her.

NELSON. Mummie, I've told you how I met the poor girl in the train, crying bitterly because her old mistress was dead and she'd nowhere to go.

MUMMIE. I don't know why she should have had to come here. Girls with good characters can always find a place, especially when they've got ankles like Alice.

NELSON. Alice's ankles had nothing to do with it. She was in distress. She wanted a situation. We wanted a maid——

MUMMIE (*hotly*). No, Nelson, that we never did.

NELSON. You mean, *you* never did.

MUMMIE. Well, the house isn't my own since she came. Wherever I go there's Alice. I get sick of her. I wish we could get rid of her. It's just fifteen shillings thrown down the gutter.

NELSON. I like that! *You* grumble about fifteen shillings for Alice—which I consider is money well spent—and yet you'll throw away five pounds on a wretched old bureau that's no good to anybody.

MUMMIE. Well, it was my own five pounds, ducksie.

NELSON. Don't argue, Mummie. It doesn't matter whose five pounds it was. It's wasted. Simply wasted. Look at the thing. All our lovely new fumed-oak furniture and you put that shabby old thing in the middle of it. It must be at least a hundred years old. I can't think what you bought it for.

MUMMIE. To keep pens and ink in.

NELSON. But you never write a letter.

MUMMIE. No, but I might want to some day. (*She leans forward eagerly.*) Besides, when you hear what I've got to tell you about that bureau——

NELSON. I don't want to hear it, thank you.

MUMMIE. But, ducksie—I must tell you. I——

NELSON. That's enough, Mummie. I won't have that bureau mentioned to me again. It spoils the whole room for me.

(She resumes her knitting.)

MUMMIE. Well, Alice spoils the whole house for me.

NELSON. Now you're just being peevish.

MUMMIE (*laying down her work again*). No, I'm not, Nelson. I don't think I trust that girl.

NELSON. Nonsense!

MUMMIE. I don't. I don't understand her. Twice I've found her on her knees by the bureau as though she was hunting for something.

NELSON. I expect the poor girl was only doing the floor.

MUMMIE. What—at twelve o'clock at night—in her nightdress?

NELSON. In her ni——? Oh.

MUMMIE (*with growing excitement*). And the other morning I caught her in my bedroom rummaging in one of my drawers. She *said* she was putting it straight. I said "Thank you, Alice," I said, "I can look after my own drawers," I said. And she turned absolutely crimson and left the room. Thank goodness I hadn't any money in that drawer.

NELSON. Mummie, *what* a thing to say. You've got your knife in poor Alice.

MUMMIE. No, I haven't, ducksie. But she does do queer things. Now why does she stay awake so late at night?

NELSON. Good gracious, Mummie. She's probably reading. Wants to improve her mind.

MUMMIE. And I'm sure she listens at doors, too. That's another thing. I dare say she's listening to us now.

NELSON. You're getting positively unhinged, Mummie!

MUMMIE. Oh, am I? Well, you tiptoe across to the door and open it suddenly and see.

NELSON. I shouldn't dream of being so silly.

MUMMIE. No, because you know it's true and you don't want to find her out.

NELSON. Well, I oughtn't to encourage you, but just to prove you're wrong, I'll do it. (*He gets up, puts his paper down and walks quietly towards the door.*)

MUMMIE (*whispering*). Quietly!

(NELSON *finishes his journey to the door on tiptoe and suddenly opens it. Outside it* ALICE *is standing.*)

NELSON (*with a gasp*). Oh! It's you, Alice.

(ALICE *comes a little way into the room. She is young, pretty, but rather pale. She has a certain "air" about her. She is in cap and dress, and at the moment is obviously a little flustered.*)

ALICE. Yes, sir. I was just coming in to know if you'd like any tea made.

NELSON (*embarrassed*). Er—would we, Mummie?

MUMMIE (*sharply*). No.

NELSON. Er—no, thank you, Alice.

ALICE. Very good, sir.

(*She goes out, closing the door quietly.*)

MUMMIE. There! You see. I told you.

NELSON (*coming back to his seat*). It was a mere accident. You heard *why* she was there.

MUMMIE. She knows we never have tea as early as this. Don't tell me. She was listening outside that door.

(*The bell rings.*)

(*Quite startled.*) Now, who's that?

NELSON. There's no need to jump like that. It's probably only the postman. It's about his time. (*He looks at his watch, which he keeps in a leather bag in his waistcoat pocket.*)

(*The door opens and* ALICE *appears on the threshold, ushering in* MRS. BOCKING.)

ALICE (*at the door*). Mrs. Bocking, please, 'm.

MRS. BOCKING (*coming in*). Oh, good morning, Mrs. Sparkes.

MUMMIE (*crossing to shake hands with her*). Hullo, Mrs. Bocking. Nice to see you. Won't you sit down?

MRS. BOCKING. Well, as a matter of fact, I came to borrow that pattern——

MUMMIE (*with extreme dignity*). That will do, Alice.

(*There is a pause while* ALICE *shuts the door.*)

NELSON. You needn't have been so sharp with her, Mummie.

MUMMIE. What does she want to stand there and gawp for?

MRS. BOCKING (*impressively*). Ah, what indeed? Mrs. Sparkes, I should get rid of that girl.

MUMMIE. So should I if it rested with me.

NELSON. Really! I can't understand women. Here's a poor, harmless, homeless, innocent girl——

MRS. BOCKING. Innocent, did you say?

NELSON (*firmly*). I did, Mrs. Bocking.

MRS. BOCKING. Then I say—poof!

NELSON. What?

MRS. BOCKING (*violently*). Poof!

NELSON. I don't quite know what you mean.

MRS. BOCKING (*impressively*). Did you have any references with that girl, Mrs. Sparkes?

MUMMIE. Oh no. Mr. Sparkes found her crying in a railway carriage and was so sorry for her he didn't *want* any references. Not that he could have had them. Her employer was dead.

MRS. BOCKING. Or never lived.

NELSON (*sternly*). Be careful, Mrs. Bocking. Be careful.

MRS. BOCKING. You be careful yourself, Mr. Sparkes, or you'll find yourself in Queer Street—or rather Bow Street—before you know where you are. (*Mysteriously.*) D'you know what that girl's *real* name is?

NELSON. Yes—Bott. Only she doesn't like it, so she calls herself Thompson.

MRS. BOCKING. She calls herself a number of things, I dare say.
But her real name is Anna Louise Kronberg, the famous International spy.

MUMMIE (*incredulously*). What—Alice?!

NELSON. Rubbish!

MRS. BOCKING. I'll show you if it's rubbish. Look at this. I cut
it out of the paper this morning. If that isn't your Alice I'll eat my
hat.

(*She exhibits a newspaper cutting which she takes from her bag.* MR.
SPARKES *gets up from his chair to examine it.*)

NELSON. Let me see, Mummie.

MUMMIE. It *is* like her.

MRS. BOCKING. Like her! It is her. You see what it says underneath.

MUMMIE. I can't see. Read it, ducksie.

NELSON (*reading slowly*). "The famous Anna Louise Kronberg,
for whom the police are searching, is believed to have stolen important papers from the Admiralty and to be in hiding. It is thought that
she may seek employment as a domestic servant and householders
are warned to be on their guard. . . ." (*There is a short amazed
silence.*) I can't believe it.

MRS. BOCKING. They say she—er—corrupted a whole regiment of
Cornish Fusiliers and all the officers are in the Tower, from the
Colonel down. But she got the papers she was after. I believe they
were hidden in a drawer in the mess.

MUMMIE. You mean Alice did all that? Why, she can't even clean
knives properly.

MRS. BOCKING. Of course she can't. *She's* no domestic servant.
She's a dangerous woman. You get rid of her quickly. Why, your
house may become the centre of a whole nest of spies.

MUMMIE (*suddenly seeing the light*). Then that's why she listens at
doors.

MRS. BOCKING (*eagerly*). Does she? Does she?

MUMMIE. Yes, we caught her just before you came in.

MRS. BOCKING. Very sinister. Very sinister indeed.

MUMMIE. And I found her down in this room one night, on her
knees, by the bureau.

MRS. BOCKING. Of course, she was probably wiring the house. I
expect it's a network of wires, so that she can hear everything that
goes on from her bedroom.

NELSON (*plaintively*). But nothing does go on.

MRS. BOCKING (*darkly*). You wait till she really gets going and has
midnight orgies in your cellar.

MUMMIE. Well, come to think of it, she does sit up very late. I've seen the light coming from under her door at one o'clock in the morning.

MRS. BOCKING. Don't you see what she's doing?

MUMMIE (*witheringly*). Mr. Sparkes says she's reading. Improving her mind.

MRS. BOCKING. Improving my aunt's hind leg! She's broadcasting, that's what she's doing.

NELSON. But where? What for?

MRS. BOCKING. Oh—telling them what goes on.

NELSON. Them? Who?

MRS. BOCKING. Oh, you know—whoever spies *do* tell. This house is probably the centre of a world-wide organization—like the Klu-Klux Klan.

MUMMIE. Whatever's that?

MRS. BOCKING. I don't know, but they wore hoods.

NELSON. Alice doesn't.

MRS. BOCKING. You don't know what she wears down in the cellar at two o'clock in the morning.

MUMMIE. I don't like it. I don't feel safe.

MRS. BOCKING. I don't wonder. I don't feel too comfortable even next door. I mean she may do anything. She may blow up the house rather than get taken alive. Spies do, you know.

MUMMIE. Oh, ducksie, *do* get rid of her—quick! I shan't sleep a wink to-night unless she's out of the house.

MRS. BOCKING. Well, I'll leave you to it. I don't feel too happy here, myself, to tell you the truth. I'll say good evening.

(MUMMIE *moves towards the bell by the fireplace.*)

No, don't ring for that Anna Louise to see me out. I'd rather go alone.

(*She whisks out of the door before anyone can follow her.*)

MUMMIE. Ducksie, my knees are going.

NELSON (*quaveringly*). So are mine. We'd better sit down, I think.

(*They sink feebly into their respective chairs.*)

MUMMIE. What *are* we to do?

NELSON. I don't know. What do you do with a famous spy?

MUMMIE (*recovering enough to get her own back*). I know what you don't do—engage her as a maid. Not if you've any sense.

NELSON. Oh, Mummie, don't gird at me.

MUMMIE. It's all very well to say don't gird, when I'm sitting over a cellarful of spies and the house is all wired.

NELSON. You don't know that it is.

MUMMIE. Well, Mrs. Bocking said it was.

NELSON. We don't even know that Alice *is* Anna Louise.

MUMMIE. Oh, don't be silly, ducksie. You saw her picture in the paper. And why did she insist on coming here?

NELSON. She certainly did insist. I wonder why? There doesn't seem anything to spy here. (*Suddenly.*) Oh, Mummie, something's just occurred to me.

MUMMIE (*breathlessly*). What? I can't bear much more, ducksie.

NELSON. She asked me to sign a paper, Alice did.

MUMMIE. You—you didn't sign it?

NELSON. Yes, I did. It was only to witness her signature.

MUMMIE. Her signature to what?

NELSON. I—I'm afraid I didn't look.

MUMMIE. Oh, Nelson! You don't know *what* you've signed. You may have sworn to blow up the Houses of Parliament.

NELSON. Oh, don't, Mummie! (*He wipes his forehead.*)

MUMMIE. You may. Or to murder poor Mr. Churchill in his bath.

NELSON. Mummie, I shall scream. (*He gets up and takes a few agitated steps across the room.*)

MUMMIE. Screaming won't get you out of Anna Louise's thrall. You'll find yourself in the Tower before you know where you are, with those officers. (*Crying.*) Oh, ducksie, I don't want you to be shot at dawn.

NELSON (*desperately*). Mummie, we've got to get rid of her—now. Will you give her notice for me? Do, Mummie. (*He comes to her and stands, looking down at her, pleadingly.*)

MUMMIE. Ducksie, I'm too frightened. If I tried to speak the notice wouldn't come out.

NELSON. Mummie, I'm afraid I've just remembered something else.

MUMMIE (*weakly*). I don't think you'd better tell me. I think my heart'll stop.

NELSON. But I must tell you, Mummie. There's no one else to tell. She gave me a parcel to leave this morning, Alice did, on my way to the office.

MUMMIE (*in a dreadful voice*). To leave where?

NELSON. For her young man—at the Admiralty, Mummie.

MUMMIE (*her eyes wide with horror*). Nelson, suppose it was a bomb.

NELSON (*with a choking cry*). Ugh! (*He clutches his hair despairingly.*)

MUMMIE. The Admiralty may be blown up by now.

NELSON. That settles it. We *must* get rid of her.

MUMMIE. But will she go?

NELSON. If she doesn't I'll threaten to inform the police.

MUMMIE. Then we may be rounded up as accomplices.

NELSON. We've got to risk it to get her out of the house.

MUMMIE. All right. I'll go and send her in to you.

NELSON (*clutching at her, desperately*). No, Mummie, don't go. Don't leave me alone with a spy. She'll tempt me. Spies always do.

MUMMIE. Don't you stand any nonsense, ducksie. If *she* tempts you, *you* tempt her back. Now, I'm going. (*She moves towards the door.*)

NELSON. No, Mummie! Mummie!

(*But* MUMMIE *has gone, shutting the door behind her.*)

(*Collapsing into his chair with a groan.*) Oh dear, oh dear, oh dear. . . . Whatever shall I say to the girl? . . . (*Sternly.*) Alice! You're a spy. . . . No, no, that's too abrupt. It'd frighten her. . . . Alice, *are* you a spy? . . . That's better, but it's a bit searching, and she might say "No" and then I'd be finished . . . I know—— (*Gently.*) Alice, why do you lead this sort of life? . . . Yes, that's it. Alice, why——

(*The door opens softly and* ALICE *comes in demurely.*)

ALICE (*just inside the door*). You sent for me, sir?

NELSON. Yes. Er—sit down.

ALICE. Thank you, sir.

(*She sits on the edge of a chair, and there ensues an awful pause during which* NELSON *clears his throat.*)

(*After a moment.*) Was there anything you wished to say to me, sir?

NELSON (*suddenly coming out with it*). Alice, why do you lead this sort of life?

ALICE (*quavering*). What sort of life do you mean, sir?

NELSON (*not quite prepared for this come-back*). Well—the sort of life you do lead. A double life, Alice.

ALICE (*tremblingly*). A double life, sir?

NELSON. Yes. You're not what you seem, are you? You had a purpose in coming here.

ALICE (*with a gasp*). How did you know?

NELSON (*taking courage from her uneasiness*). Never mind how. I do know.

ALICE (*breaking down*). I didn't mean any harm, sir. Really I didn't.

NELSON (*outraged*). Not mean any harm! How can you sit there and say such a thing?

ALICE. I wanted the money, sir.

NELSON. You depraved girl.

ALICE. Well, a hundred pounds means a lot to me, sir, and you didn't know it was there.

NELSON (*at sea*). Didn't know it was where?

ALICE. In the bureau—the one Mrs. Sparkes bought at the sale.

NELSON. I don't understand. What was in the bureau?

ALICE (*crying*). A hundred pounds.

NELSON. Are you telling me that there's a hundred pounds in that bureau?

ALICE. Yes—in the secret drawer.

NELSON. Nonsense! Who put it there?

ALICE (*snivelling*). Mrs. Stott.

NELSON. Whoever's Mrs. Stott?

ALICE. The lady the desk belonged to—my mistress. She hid it there. I saw her. And when her things were sold I found out that Mrs. Sparkes had bought it, and I made up my mind to get in here somehow and find it.

NELSON. I don't believe a word of it.

ALICE. It's true. If you look in the desk you'll see it's true.

NELSON. Show me where it is, then!

ALICE. I can't open it. Mrs. Sparkes has the key.

NELSON. Oh, you know that, do you? Well, we'll soon get the key. (*Going to the door and calling.*) Mummie!

MUMMIE (*who has evidently been waiting just outside the door— coming in at once—tremulously*). Yes, ducksie?

NELSON. Have you got the key of this bureau?

MUMMIE. Yes, ducksie. Here it is in my bag. Why? (*She hands him a key from her bag.*)

NELSON. Give it to me. This girl's trying to fob me off with a cock-and-bull story of there being a hundred pounds hidden in a secret drawer. Now then, we'll soon find out.

(*He strides to the bureau and unlocks it with a stern air.* ALICE *rises eagerly.*)

Now, Alice—or whatever your name is—where's the drawer?

ALICE (*coming over to him*). Wait till I get my finger on the right spot.

MUMMIE (*approaching too*). You wicked girl. How did you know there *was* a drawer?

NELSON. Quiet a minute, Mummie. Well, Alice?

ALICE. Here! (*She puts her hand inside the bureau and pulls out a secret drawer.*)

NELSON (*aside to* MUMMIE). There is a drawer, Mummie.

ALICE (*bursting into tears*). The hundred pounds isn't there!

NELSON (*in righteous wrath*). Of course it isn't. It never was there. The whole thing was a lie. You thought you'd try and hoodwink me, didn't you? It's no use, Alice. I know what you are—*who* you are. You're a spy! Anna Louise Kronberg, that's who you are. Ah, you're surprised, aren't you? I told you I knew everything.

ALICE (*weeping copiously*). But I—I——

NELSON (*commandingly*). That's enough. Out of the house you go.

ALICE. Oh, sir, I——

NELSON. Ssh! I won't hear any more. You go and spy somewhere else. Go on, go on, go on!

(*He shoos the weeping, miserable* ALICE *out of the room and closes the door after her with finality.*)

(*Sitting down again with relief.*) Well, that's got rid of her. I don't think she's much of a spy, Mummie. She broke down completely under my cross-examination. Fancy expecting me to believe that there was a hundred pounds in a bureau drawer.

MUMMIE (*quietly*). But there was, ducksie.

NELSON. What!

MUMMIE. There *was* a hundred pounds there.

NELSON. Then where is it?

MUMMIE. In the Post Office Savings Bank.

NELSON. Who put it there?

MUMMIE. I did.

NELSON. And you never told me a word about it, Mummie ; how deceitful.

MUMMIE (*meekly*). I didn't mean to be, ducksie. I did try to tell you, but you wouldn't let me mention the bureau. You were so angry when I bought it and every time I tried to bring the subject up you snapped at me.

NELSON. Yes, but I didn't know there was a hundred pounds in it. Now, Mummie, you go straight down to the Post Office in the morning and get that money and give it to me.

MUMMIE (*meekly*). Yes, ducksie. And shall I go and tell Alice she isn't a spy, after all?

NELSON. Certainly not. Why should Alice know everything?

MUMMIE. I just thought——

NELSON. Well, don't think. You never were any good at it. See where your thinking nearly brought us to-day.

MUMMIE (*properly ashamed of herself*). I'm sorry, ducksie. I won't think any more.

NELSON. Good. Now I'll just go and enter that hundred pounds in my cash-book. (*He rises and stands contemplating the bureau.*) You know, Mummie, that's not a bad bureau. I said at the time— don't you remember?—what a good bit of walnut it was. I think I'll keep my papers in it. . . .

The CURTAIN *falls.*